The Forgo

- the life and legacies of Sir Francis Galton

David Allen, CBE MPhil

Table of contents

Preface

A couple of birthdays ago, I was given a copy of a book by Leonard Mlodinow, entitled *The Drunkard's Walk*. This was about randomness and probabilities and, towards the end of the book, the author acknowledged the contribution of one Sir Francis Galton to the development of interpretive statistics.

I had studied statistics on the road to acquiring the National Certificate in Commerce, and membership of what is now the Chartered Institute of Management Accountants, and was familiar with the techniques mentioned – but none of my lecturers or textbooks had covered their origins or given credit to their discoverers / inventors.

Given my Black Country upbringing, the name Galton rang a bell, since I knew of the achievements of Samuel Galton Junior, a member of the Lunar Society towards the end of the eighteenth century, and the beginning of the nineteenth. Fellow members included Erasmus Darwin and Matthew Boulton (the founders), James Watt, Josiah Wedgwood and Joseph Priestly. Collectively, the members of the Society had been responsible for some of the most important advances in science, industry and commerce.

In particular, Samuel Galton Junior was a successful Quaker businessman, playing a major role in the development of manufacturing, banking, and the Birmingham Navigation sector of the British canal network – commemorated in the naming of Galton Valley and its museum, and Galton Bridge and its railway station. Was Sir Francis Galton any relation?

Indeed he was. Born in the Sparkbrook area of Birmingham in 1822, he was the grandson, not only of Samuel Galton Junior, but see that *his* ideas – as distinct from those of the people claiming to be his followers - are as relevant today as when he published them.

Ironically, the Fabians dominated the U.K. parliament that was elected at the end of the Second World War, and were able to introduce their version of national socialism by way of the most radical political shift in the nation's history. With one exception, subsequent governments have presided over a drift to the left of the political spectrum, as universal suffrage prompts politicians to do what will appeal to the masses, rather than the elite. Only the European Commissioners carry the torch for the idea of government by a bureaucratic elite, thanks to their immunity from such distractions as elections.

The consequences of this drift are exactly as one would predict from an understanding of Galton's work, most notably the following.

- The world population has more than tripled in the century since Galton's death, with the major growth being in the poorer countries.
- The U.K. government is unable to make ends meet, as demand for benefits, and services that are free at the point of delivery, outstrips the supply that can be funded from taxation (its current borrowings are around £1.4 trillion and rising).
- Poverty, housing shortages and troubled families are serious issues, overarched by the effects of an unprecedented level of immigration.
- The adoption of a 'comprehensive' approach to education has led to a levelling down in state schools, exacerbating the gap between their results and those of the private schools.

Meanwhile, however, surgical and pharmaceutical developments have made it more feasible to take actions which have a eugenic feel about them. Contraception, abortion, and in vitro fertilisation

4

(allowing screening of embryos) are now commonplace, life expectancy has increased enormously, and euthanasia and assisted dying are current topics. The point is that the underlying ideas of eugenics, as originally promulgated by Galton, are a valid input to informed debate on such topics.

The layout of this book is roughly chronological, starting with Galton's life: his background, education and his discoveries in various fields, followed by a focus on his work on heredity and eugenics. Then we shall cover his (albeit unintended) legacies in the shape of the extensions of the philosophy and practice of eugenics by intellectuals and dictators (the ultimate elite!), and the post-war developments in politics, medicine, education and migration, before concluding with a look at the current scene.

Along the way, I am hoping that you will agree that Sir Francis Galton's achievements are worthy of acclaim, and that that his reputation is worthy of rehabilitation.

David Allen, Solihull, 2014

About the author

David Allen, CBE. MPhil, has now retired after a career in industry, which began as a commercial apprentice with a Black Country engineering group, and the highlight of which was as financial director of Cadbury Ltd., based in Bournville, Birmingham. Thereafter he took on various non-executive roles in both the private and public sectors.

He is a Fellow and a past president of the Chartered Institute of Management Accountants, and a Fellow of the Institute of Chartered Secretaries and of the Royal Society of Arts. He was for ten years a visiting professor at Loughborough University Business School, where his specialist topic was Strategic Financial Management. He was awarded the CBE in recognition of his contribution to the world wide accountancy profession by way of his work for the International Federation of Accountants.

In retirement, he was the founder treasurer (and later chairman) of Blossomfield (Solihull) U3A, and took particular pleasure in setting up its History Group, which continues to thrive. The first 'outing' of the material in this book was as a lecture to that group, which led on to similar presentations to the full U3A membership and, indeed, to other U3As, history societies, church groups and the like. The response he has received at these talks has prompted him to elaborate the ideas into this book.

All proceeds from the talks and royalties from the sale of this book are donated to Canine Partners, a charity which trains assistance dogs for the disabled.

1. A rich inheritance

Brummie pioneers

I guess that every generation feels that the rate of change it is experiencing is the fastest ever – and perhaps that is right, in that it is exponential. One period that might claim to be particularly outstanding, however, was that which coincided with the reign of George III, i.e. between 1760 and 1820. For Great Britain, this was the time of the loss of the American colonies, the ultimately successful wars against Napoleonic France, and the world's first Industrial Revolution.

The reason the last mentioned occurred at that time, and in Great Britain rather than anywhere else, is down to the coming together of a number of strands, notably:

- natural advantages, including a favourable climate and the abundance of key raw materials, such as coal, ironstone and limestone;

- a growing industrial workforce, created by the exodus from the land which resulted from improvements in agriculture, such as Jethro Tull's seed drill;

- substantial wealth, in relatively few hands, thanks to the profits made from agriculture and overseas ventures, aided by very low taxation of personal and corporate income;

- an efficiently operating market economy, and a culture in which ideas were freely exchanged;

- a cadre of people with the requisite knowledge, intelligence, creativity and work ethic needed to establish enterprises and to attract the necessary capital.

Predominant among those pioneers was a Midlands-based group known as the Lunar Society (in recognition of their practice of meeting on the Monday nearest each full moon, to aid their homeward journeys). At the time, Birmingham had become a hot-house of innovation and development, attracting many enthusiastic and energetic people from all over the country. This had come about because, not being a chartered town, and having no craft guilds, it was free of such restrictions as:

- the Clarendon Code (1660's) and the Test Acts (1670's) which re-established the supremacy of the Anglican Church and effectively prevented both Catholics and dissenters from worshipping in chartered towns;

- the craft guilds' closed shops for various trades, entered only by way of long apprenticeships.

It is also noteworthy that it had no parliamentary representation at that time. That did not come about until the 1832 Reform Act, amongst the agitators for which were the members of the Birmingham Political Union led by Thomas Attwood, who became the town's first Member of Parliament.

Among the most well-known members of the Lunar Society were the following, all of them members of the Royal Society, which had been formed in 1660, with the emphasis on experiment and making discoveries. Its motto *Nullius in verba* is roughly translated as 'take nobody's word'.

Josiah Wedgwood FRS 1730 – 1795 is well known for his pottery, having achieved prominence with a cream coloured tea and coffee service for Queen Charlotte. He was a pioneer of modern management: separating the 'useful' and 'ornamental' businesses, complete with their own administration, etc.; breaking jobs down into small stages and training otherwise unskilled workers; and developing functions now known as management accounting (e.g. recognising the variability of cost, and measuring product profitability) and marketing (e.g. royal endorsement).

However, like the other Lunar men, he had a wide range of interests, and usually took a leading role, as with the first long distance canal (the Grand Trunk, now known as the Trent and Mersey) his original motive being to reduce the damage to his finished products in transit (but it also helped with raw materials from Cheshire and via Liverpool). He was an active member of the Unitarian Church, and a leading light in the campaign against slavery - producing and giving away large numbers of a medallion inscribed 'Am I not a man and a brother?' He was also the prime mover in the creation of the first General Chamber of Commerce.

Erasmus Darwin FRS 1731 – 1802, was born and grew up in Newark, obtained degrees from Cambridge and Edinburgh, and spent many years in Lichfield, before moving to Derby. A twenty stone doctor, who turned down the opportunity to be the King's personal physician, he was a highly regarded poet. He was also a successful naturalist: identifying the process of photosynthesis, and sketching out a hypothesis of evolution in *The laws of organic life*, (which was to be famously evidenced, elaborated and elevated to the status of a theory by his grandson Charles). He wrote extensively on clouds, and identified 'weather fronts' (meetings of two masses of air of different densities, classified as warm, cold or occluded) as the principal cause of meteorological phenomena (such as the rain experienced in the United Kingdom) a concept still crucial to weather forecasting to this day. He was also an innovative engineer, including his design of the steering system for carriages (but still used in modern cars), of speaking and copying machines, and an early rocket engine. His Lichfield home now comprises a visitor attraction and study centre.

Joseph Priestley FRS, 1733 – 1804, is probably most well known as a chemist, especially for his work on air in its various forms: the isolation and understanding of oxygen; the identification of the constituents of water; the invention of soda water (but he let Jacob Schweppe make his fortune from its exploitation) and the recognition that plants took in carbon dioxide and gave out oxygen.

Meanwhile, he was a dissenting minister, a founder of the British branch of Unitarianism, and a tutor at the Dissenting Academy in Warrington. He promoted the idea that a study of history furthered the understanding of God's natural laws. He was also a political reformist and, on account of his perceived sympathies with the French Revolution, his house (bought from Sampson Lloyd of the banking family) at Fair Hill in Sparkbrook, Birmingham was burned down by rioters in 1791. The site is now 10 Priestley Road, marked by a plaque. He was sheltered by the Galtons in the immediate aftermath of the fire, but later moved to Pennsylvania.

James Watt FRS 1736 – 1819, a Scottish engineer, is most famous for having made enormous improvements on Newcomen's steam engine, in terms of cost and efficiency, by incorporating a separate condenser. A Presbyterian, it is said that he was motivated by the desire to minimise the waste of material (coal) which had been provided by God for man's use.

Later, he also found a way to convert horizontal energy into rotary, which was to widen the market away from pumping (notably mines in Cornwall) to all kinds of manufacturing. In order to describe the capability of his engines to prospective customers, he invented the concept of 'horsepower' (one horsepower being 33,000 foot-pounds per minute) and is remembered in terms of his name being used as the term describing the rate of energy conversion (one watt equalling one joule per second). He also invented a chemically treated paper for duplicating, which dominated the market until the arrival of carbon paper. He was prone to depression and disillusionment, but was helped by Matthew Boulton and William Murdock (the pioneer of gas lighting and steam locomotion but never a member of the Lunar Society) to overcome it.

Matthew Boulton FRS 1728 – 1809 married twice into the Robinson family, who were based in Lichfield, and were patients of Doctor Erasmus Darwin. Boulton was an entrepreneur based at Soho House and Soho Foundry, the latter accommodating a thousand workers (rather than using outworkers, as was the general practice up until that time), making everything from buttons through coins to steam engines. Soho House is now a visitor centre under the auspices of Birmingham Museums. In 1773, he successfully lobbied for the authorisation of the Birmingham Assay office.

In the 1770s, when the collapse of a Scottish bank led to the bankruptcy of James Watt's financial backer, Boulton took a two-thirds interest in the development of the steam engine. With additional help from Joseph Priestley's brother in law, John ('Iron Mad') Wilkinson, Boulton and Watt brought out the first working models in 1776 (the oldest still in working order being in Birmingham's Science Museum 'Thinktank'). Boulton was very alert to the value of what we now call 'intellectual property' and succeeded in getting the patent extended, which gave the firm a virtual monopoly for many years. Their position was further strengthened by their strategy of asking for payment for the engines, not as a lump sum, but on the basis of one third of the energy cost savings.

Boulton saw mechanisation as the way to reduce costs and ensure consistency, and established the first steam powered Mint, producing the British copper coinage, standardised coins for many parts of the world, commemorative medals, and customised tokens for businesses. He also introduced works committees and an insurance club. In a letter to Samuel Johnson, James Boswell quoted Boulton as saying 'I sell here, sir, what all the world desires: power'.

Boulton (together with that quote) and Watt are pictured on the current £50 note. On launching the new design in 2010, the Governor of the Bank of England (now Lord King of Lothbury) commented that 'The partnership of an innovator and an entrepreneur created exactly the kind of commercial success that we will need in this country as we rebalance our economy over the years ahead'.

The two pioneers are also, together with William Murdock, commemorated in a statue created by William Bloye, and erected in 1956, in Broad Street, Birmingham. It is known locally as 'the golden boys'.

Samuel Galton Junior, FRS, 1753 – 1832, was born in Duddeston, Birmingham to Samuel Galton senior and Mary, nee Farmer, both from Quaker families (the Galtons having moved from Bristol in the 1740's). After a spell at Warrington Academy, he returned to Birmingham at the age of 21, to take responsibility for the family businesses, the main one involving the manufacture of guns, which were supplied to merchants in Bristol who then exchanged them for slaves on the west coast of Africa. In 1777 he married Lucy Barclay of the banking family.

From 1785 to 1799, they rented Great Barr Hall from the Scott family, and this became a favourite meeting place of the Lunar Society. Interestingly, in view of what we shall see when we look at the work of his grandson Francis, it was bought in 1910 by the West Bromwich Poor Law Guardians, and used as the Great Barr Idiot Colony (looking after 'imbeciles, idiots and the feeble minded'). Renamed as St Margaret's Hospital, it carried on this work until the nineteen eighties but it is now derelict, following a fire on the day that Bovis Homes began to develop the neighbouring land for executive housing.

Samuel found it increasingly difficult to reconcile his Quakerism with his gun making. He argued that what his customers did with his products was their business – the guns might even prevent conflict - but this did not convince his fellows, and he was expelled from the Birmingham Society of Friends in 1796 for 'fabricating instruments for the destruction of mankind'.

He was, however, a very successful businessman, including investments in agriculture and property. He was a shareholder in the Birmingham Canal Navigation (like Wedgwood, his original motive was to reduce damage in transit, but the investment turned out to be very profitable) and is commemorated in Galton Bridge and Galton Valley Canal Museum. He and his father funded much of Priestley's work.

He was a statistician before that term was invented, often expressing business data in bar charts and graphs for easier assimilation. He was also interested in science, especially light, optics and colour.

As early as 1672, Sir Isaac Newton had shown how white light can be decomposed into a spectrum of colours by being passed through a prism. He used this discovery to explain the rainbow, its seven colours conveniently harmonising with musical notation, the

Sun plus the then known planets, and the days of the week. Newton also discovered that the seven colours could be recomposed into white, a fact which he demonstrated by passing them through another prism, or painting them on to a rotating wheel.

Samuel Galton junior, however, spotted what is obvious to us, namely that four of Newton's colours (orange, green, indigo and violet) were combinations of others. Hence, in a paper presented to the Royal Society in 1782 but not published until 1799, he showed (again by way of a rotating wheel) that white light could be produced equally well by mixing just three colours - red, blue and yellow – in the right proportions. He had identified what we now know as the primary colours, an achievement commemorated on his 'moonstone' (alongside ones for seven other Lunar Men) outside the ASDA store in Queslett, Birmingham. In 1804, he handed over responsibility for his businesses to his son, Samuel Tertius Galton.

Samuel Galton Junior took over Duddeston House in 1799 on the death of his father, where he lived for the rest of his life. When the Lunar Society disbanded in 1813, he purchased its collection of papers.

A growing family

As well as interaction within the group, the members of the Lunar Society were also in touch with people in other fields, such as Joseph Banks, the plant hunter; John Baskerville, the printer; James Boswell, the biographer of Samuel Johnson; James Cook, the explorer (who obtained various trinkets from Boulton to exchange with natives); William Hutton, the self-educated historian (whose house was also burned down in the riots of 1791);

Joseph Wright, the painter (who produced portraits of many of the Lunar men, and various industrial scenes).

There were several marriages between members of the families of the Lunar men, with those most relevant to this book being as follows:

- Robert Darwin, a son of Erasmus Darwin and Mary nee Howard, married Josiah Wedgwood's daughter Susannah, and one of their children was Charles Darwin (who married Emma Wedgwood, daughter of Josiah II).

- Violetta (1783 – 1874), a daughter of Erasmus Darwin and Elizabeth Pole, married **Samuel Tertius Galton (1783 – 1844)**, the son of Samuel Galton junior and Lucy nee Barclay in 1807, and one of their children was Francis Galton.

From this, we see that our subject, Francis Galton, and the more celebrated Charles Darwin, of 'Origin of Species' and 'Descent of Man' fame, were half-cousins, Erasmus Darwin being the grandfather of both.

Samuel Tertius Galton was very interested in economics, and published a paper in 1813 on the relationships between the money supply, the general price level and the exchange rate, summed up as follows: 'The chart shows that every great movement by any one line is accompanied by a variation nearly simultaneously of the others .... It is impossible to resist the inference that the same cause has operated upon them all. This tendency towards parallelism ...'

He did not speculate on the cause that operated on the variables, but did warn of the danger of inconvertible money getting out of control. That idea seemed to remain dormant until the 1980's when Milton Friedman argued that the Federal

Reserve's restriction of the money supply in the 1920's had brought on deflation, and exacerbated the depression. Nigel Lawson, Chancellor of the Exchequer in Margaret Thatcher's cabinet, was a follower, declaring that 'inflation is a monetary phenomenon'. Likewise the 'Quantitative Easing' initiated in 2008 was clearly a move designed to avoid a repetition of the experience of the 1920's as described by Friedman, albeit accepting the accompanying debasement of the currency (reflected in inflation and a deteriorating exchange rate).

In 1814, Samuel Tertius was appointed to the post of High Bailiff of Birmingham and, shortly thereafter, disposed of the gun business, and converted to the Church of England denomination. Between 1820 and 1831, he rented 'The Larches' in Sparkbrook (close to where Joseph Priestley had lived) from the son of another Lunar Society member William Withering. Then, in 1831, he disposed of the bank, and moved to Leamington (where he was a magistrate) with a country house in Claverdon (later developed as the Ardencote Manor hotel). He died in 1844, leaving a substantial fortune.

Francis Galton 1822 - 1911

The net result of all this is that we see that the youngest of Samuel Tertius's seven children, Francis, clearly came from very good stock (and, indeed, saw himself as an heir to the scientific and intellectual tradition represented by the Lunar Society). He was something of a child prodigy, learning the alphabet at eighteen months, reading at the age of two and a half, reciting long poems at five, and discussing Greek literature before starting school. This was enhanced by his formal education, as follows:

- 1830 – 2, Boarding school in Boulogne;

- 1832 – 5, Reverend Attwood's School in Kenilworth;

- 1835 – 8, King Edward V1 School in Birmingham;

- 1838 – 9, Birmingham General Hospital;

- 1839 – 40, King's College Medical School (did his mother hope that he would emulate her father?);

- 1840 – 44, Trinity College Cambridge, where he studied mathematics.

Cambridge was very difficult for him and, following a nervous breakdown, he gained only a 'poll' degree. One thing he observed whilst there was how often someone who was very good at a particular subject, such as mathematics, had a relative (more often than not a father) who was also very good at it – and this was to be reflected later in his thoughts and publications on the subject of heredity. It was just as he was leaving Cambridge that his father died, leaving Francis an inheritance so substantial that he would have no need to earn money, but could pursue his own interests.

Francis Galton was knighted in 1909 and died in 1911 in Haslemere, but was buried in the family grave at Claverdon, where a plaque in the church reads: 'Many branches of science owe much to his labours but the dominant idea of his life's work was to measure the influence of heredity on the mental and physical attributes of mankind'.

I hope to show, in the following pages, that this is a considerable understatement.

2. Galton the polymath

As mentioned at the end of the previous chapter, Francis Galton's primary interest was in heredity, but this overlapped with work on statistics, psychology and eugenics. Before examining any of those topics, however, it is worth looking at yet other fields in which he made significant contributions.

Exploration

A portent of how his life would progress can be gleaned from Francis's interest, around the time he left Cambridge University, in phrenology. This professed science was rooted in the idea that a minute examination of the shape of a person's skull, including its 'lumps and bumps', could provide an indication of his or her intelligence and character. It was very popular throughout the nineteenth century – the leading textbook on the subject ran to eleven editions.

In 1849, after living the life of a country squire for a while - augmented by trips to Europe, Egypt, The Holy Land and the Sudan - Francis consulted a leading phrenologist, Cornelius Donovan PhD, who advised him that he had the capacity to rough it in a colonisation environment, advice which Francis followed with enthusiasm.

With support (in the form of introductions etc., not finance) from the Royal Geographical Society ('RGS'), he spent the period from August 1850 until January 1852 in Damaraland and Ovampoland (parts of what is now the Republic of Namibia). He led a party of nearly forty men on a journey he described as 'a tedious and anxious one, but happily brought to a close without loss of life or serious injury'. He noted that the journey had helped to develop 'habits of self-reliance in rude emergencies, which are well worth possessing'.

Using a sextant, compass, and his knowledge of astronomy and trigonometry, he was able to create the first accurate map of any part of Africa, describing the topography - including latitude, longitude, altitude and distances between features - which, in turn, helped to open up the country to commerce.

A year after his return, he published his *Narrative of an explorer in Tropical South Africa – shifts and contrivances available in wild countries*, in recognition of which the RGS awarded him its gold medal. Presenting the medal, the president referred to his work in 'a country never before penetrated by a civilised being'. Portuguese explorers had reached its shores in the fifteenth century but had not moved inland, and had not laid any claims.

A foretaste of his views on ethnicity appeared in that publication, in a reference to some of the natives being 'a sort of link to civilisation'. He was later to say that 'I saw enough of savage races to give me material for the rest of my life'. However, we need to bear in mind, in respect of this and other examples of Francis's work, that the conventional wisdom in Victorian times did not include seeing all men as having been created equal. At home, the prevailing social hierarchy was seen as a reflection of an underlying natural order: the poor being intrinsically inferior to the rich. As far as 'abroad' was concerned, the view was that Africans had not reached European levels of sophistication because they were naturally inferior.

Namibia has had a chequered history since then:

- It became a German protectorate ('German South West Africa') in 1884, the first Governor being Heinrich Goering, the father of Hermann. There were difficulties, culminating in an uprising in 1904, which prompted an 'Extermination Order', as a result of which at least a hundred thousand Herero and

Namaqua people were killed (the officers in charge of which were decorated by the Kaiser). This gave rise to the first use of the expression 'concentration camp' in which the racial biologist Eugen Fischer carried out 'experiments' in support of his theories about the dangers of racial mixture - atrocities that were forerunners of Nazi 'racial hygiene' policies.

- In 1915, the 6,000 German troops in Namibia were overwhelmed by a 60,000 strong South African force. Tons of equipment were dumped in the 80 metre deep Lake Otjikoto – and, it is believed, so was a safe containing tens of millions of pounds worth of gold and diamonds. Not surprisingly, it continues to be very popular with divers. From then until its independence in 1990, Namibia was under the control of South Africa and subject to its white supremacy policies and laws.

- These days, though one of the world's most sparsely populated countries (2.2 people per square kilometre), it is nevertheless a popular 'package holiday' destination, with Galton House in Windhoek (the capital) offering a base for safaris.

Galton's reputation in the area is evidenced by the naming of a plant, native to Southern Africa, in his honour: the Galtonia (its popular name being the summer hyacinth).

Consolidation

On the first of August 1853, Francis married Louisa Butler (sister of the Master of Trinity College Cambridge, daughter of the Dean of Peterborough Cathedral, and later to be the great aunt of leading Conservative politician R. A. Butler). They spent the rest of that year honeymooning in Switzerland, Italy and France, before setting up home in Rutland Gate, London.

Over the next few years, he:

20

- was elected to the Council (and, later, became Honorary Secretary) of the RGS;

- became a member (and, later, a vice president) of the Royal Statistical Society;

- was invited to join the Athenaeum club;

- edited *Hints to Travellers* combining his own and others' experiences, which went on through numerous reprints to become RGS's most popular book;

- published an elaboration of *Hints*, called *The Art of Travel* and was invited by the then Prime Minister (Lord Palmerston) to run a series of seminars for the army – elements of which can still be found in military curricula;

- was very active in the British Association for the Advancement of Science (including a spell as General Secretary);

- campaigned, successfully, to get geography on school curricula;

- was elected a Fellow of the Royal Society;

- joined the management committee (and later became chairman) of the Kew Observatory.

Some networking!

Meteorology

As we saw in the previous chapter, Francis Galton's maternal grandfather, Erasmus Darwin, had been the first to explain weather fronts. He had gone on to describe how they influence our weather: warm fronts moving between north and south, and characterised by fog; cold fronts moving between west and east, and characterised by severe weather, e.g. thunderstorms. He also advocated the plotting of 'weather maps' but these had to wait for the involvement of his grandson.

Specifically, that milestone arose from the responsibilities of Vice Admiral Robert Fitzroy (1805 – 1865) formerly captain of the 'Beagle' and governor of New Zealand. By 1860, he was head of the meteorology department of government (the forerunner of the Meteorological Office) and had embarked on the task of collecting data, in the hope that he would be able to discern some patterns which would aid weather forecasting.

To help him, Francis Galton wrote to meteorologists in 80 stations all over Europe, asking them for various readings (wind, cloud, pressure, temperature, moisture) three times a day, for the month of December 1861. He published his experience in June 1863 in a book called 'Meteorographica' – a word he coined to describe a two-fold process:

- the art and practice of tabulating observations which have been made simultaneously at numerous stations; and

- subsequently, delineating the results in pictorial form, which made their meaning apparent at a glance – as with a map produced from data about longitudes, latitudes, etc.

What he did was to plot the information from those 80 stations in the form of 'weather charts' of his own design and, from a comparison of the readings, he was able to see how weather patterns developed. Amongst his observations were:

- the frequent wind currents sweeping across the charts, being part of enormous systems beyond the boundaries of his maps;

- the simultaneity of wind changes across the whole system;

- the shallowness of the lowest stratum of the atmosphere, evidenced by the diverting power of mountains;

- the existence of anticyclones (another word he coined), namely large scale circulations of winds around a central region of high pressure, clockwise in the northern hemisphere (but later observed to be anticlockwise in the southern). It is associated with clear skies, and settled, cool, dry air.

He acknowledged that data over a wider area and a longer period would be required to advance the knowledge so gained (what would he make of the massive computer power available to today's Meteorological Office?) but he maintained an interest, being a member of the Meteorological Council for many years. Meanwhile, he invented various pieces of weather measuring equipment. He prepared the very first weather map for general publication as soon as printing technology allowed (in *The Times* on the 1st of April 1875) showing isobars (yet another word he coined, to describe lines of equal barometric pressure) temperatures, the state of sea and sky, and wind directions for the previous day. The format is still in use.

Fingerprint identification

A fingerprint is an impression of the friction ridges of a finger, which may be left:

- by the natural secretions of sweat; or

- by ink or other substances on a smooth surface.

Fingerprints have been found in relics from ancient Babylon, Egypt and China. They were being used in India in 1858 by Sir

William Herschel (grandson of the man of the same name - 'the musician of Bath' - who discovered Uranus in 1781). In Hooghly, near Calcutta, he introduced them on contracts and deeds, to prevent the then rampant repudiation of written signatures. He also registered pensioners' fingerprints to prevent relatives continuing to collect pensions after the beneficiaries' deaths, and built up a file of prisoners' fingerprints.

Then, in 1880, Dr Henry Faulds, a Scottish surgeon working in a Tokyo hospital sent a letter to *Nature,* discussing the usefulness of fingerprints for identification, and going on to propose a method to record them with printing ink. Returning to the UK in 1886, he described his system in a letter to Charles Darwin, who passed it to Francis Galton, who was too busy on other work at the time, and passed it to the Royal Anthropological Society.

In 1888, however, Galton's attention was drawn back to the subject while preparing a lecture on 'personal identification' for the Royal Institution. Having made inquiries, he described himself as 'surprised to find, both how much had been done, and how much there remained to do, before establishing their theoretical value and practical utility'. He had thought (even hoped?) that there might be some connection with heredity and eminence, but this was not to be. He obtained records from Herschel, and studied over 8,000 prints taken in his anthropometric laboratory before publishing *Finger Prints,* in 1892, in which he:

- showed that they were unique to each individual, a surer criterion of identity than any other bodily feature, and that they did not change significantly with age;

- described a detailed statistical model of fingerprint analysis and identification, later elaborated by Sir Edward Henry, but many of the basic characteristics are still in use today, and often referred to as 'Galton Details';

- calculated that the chance of a 'false positive' (two different individuals having the same fingerprints) was about 1 in 64 billion; and

- encouraged their use in forensic science.

This prepared the way for the positive findings of the Parliamentary committee chaired by Herbert Asquith in 1894, which led to the acceptance of fingerprint testimony in the courts. Further, in 1901, a fingerprint bureau was established at Scotland Yard.

Other ideas

Being mentally hyperactive, Galton worried lest his brain overheat, so he built a bulb-operated lid on his top hat. He also invented:

- a gumption reviver, which was a dripping tap above his head;

- prescription goggles, so that he could read in his bath;

- a bicycle speedometer (not very popular as it was based on an egg timer).

He also initiated the idea of composite photos, so as to express the average appearance of different groups, but with potential for other applications.

All of the above give an impression of the range of his interests, but we now turn to his core activity, starting with his pioneering work in statistics, motivated by his desire to provide evidence for his theories on heredity.

3. Statistics

Influences

One of Isaac Newton's most memorable utterances was his comment that his achievements were not all that remarkable once it was acknowledged that he had been 'standing on the shoulders of giants', such as Galileo Galilei.

Francis Galton was one of the pioneers of modern statistics, especially the inquisitive and interpretative aspects, as he sought sound evidence in his work on heredity (developing techniques that were later picked up in many aspects of biology). In his case, too, it is worth highlighting some of the earlier discoveries on which he was able to build.

They were primarily concerned with the quantification of 'chance', and underpin the concept of 'probability'. Take the tossing of two coins, for example. There are four possible outcomes: head + head, head + tail, tail + head, tail plus tail. The more times they are tossed, the closer will be the pattern of results to one in which the combination head + tail (or its equivalent, tail + head) occurs 50% of the time, and the others 25% each. As we shall see later, even in this simple form, that realisation was crucial to the discovery, by Gregor Mendel, of the progress of genes.

More generally, however, it was expressed as a mathematical formula known as the binomial theorem. Readers will, perhaps, be familiar with the algebra:

$$(a + b)^2 = a^2 + 2ab + b^2$$

$$(a + b)^3 = a^3 + 3a^2b + 3ab^2 + b^3$$

$$(a + b)^4 = a^4 + 4a^3b + 6a^2b^2 + 4ab^3 + b^4$$

and so on.

If the coefficients of the various terms are displayed as an array, we obtain what is known as Pascal's Triangle (named for the French physicist Blaise Pascal, 1623 – 62) in which each coefficient is the sum of the two straddling it in the row above, as follows:

$$1$$

$$1 \quad 1$$

$$1 \quad 2 \quad 1$$

$$1 \quad 3 \quad 3 \quad 1$$

$$1 \quad 4 \quad 6 \quad 4 \quad 1$$

$$1 \quad 5 \quad 10 \quad 10 \quad 5 \quad 1$$

$$1 \quad 6 \quad 15 \quad 20 \quad 15 \quad 6 \quad 1$$

and so on

Francis Galton devised a mechanical way of demonstrating this, which he called the Quincunx, but is more widely known as the Galton Board. This comprises an upright board with a triangular array of evenly placed pegs. Balls are dropped on to the top peg, and bounce their way down to the bottom, where they are collected in slots. Given an equal chance of bouncing left or right from each peg they encounter, the balls collect in the pegs in a pattern which tends towards that of Pascal's Triangle.

I stress 'tends' because one must avoid the presumption that in an individual experiment involving, say, 32 tosses, the result will be exactly $1 - 5 - 10 - 10 - 5 - 1$, but the larger the number of tosses, the closer to that pattern will be the outcome.

The results can be expressed in the form of a histogram but, again, the greater the number of tosses, the closer the distribution will resemble a curve, which is known by various names:

- the Gaussian curve - named for the German mathematician Carl Friedrich Gauss, 1777 – 1855;
- or, because of its shape, the bell curve;
- or, because of its ubiquity, the normal curve.

Having read mathematics at Cambridge, Francis Galton was familiar with the works of Pascal and Gauss, but was also influenced by two other writers, as follows.

David Hume, 1711 – 1776, was a Scottish philosopher, historian and economist, who endeavoured – starting with his *Treatise on human nature* - to create a comprehensive naturalistic 'science of man' that examined the psychological basis of human nature.   He advocated experience and observation as the foundation for logical argument, aiming to adapt the methodology of Newtonian physics and thereby 'extend our conquest over all those sciences which more intimately concern human life'. As we shall see, however, whereas physics majored on certainties, the social sciences (along with biology) needed the arrival of a new approach, namely a probability-based concept of statistics.

In economics, Hume favoured private property, given that resources are finite; were they not, he argued, private property would be 'an idle ceremonial'. He also believed in the unequal distribution of wealth, on the grounds that perfect equality would destroy the concepts of thrift and industry, and lead to impoverishment.

Adolphe Quetelet, 1796 – 1874, was the Belgian Astronomer Royal, and was instrumental in introducing statistical method to the social sciences – what he called 'social physics'. His goal was to understand the statistical laws underlying such phenomena as crime rates, marriage rates or suicide rates. He wanted to explain the values of these variables by reference to other social factors. These ideas were rather controversial, in that some scientists held that they contradicted the concept of God-given freedom of choice.

Nevertheless, Quetelet found strong relationships between crime and such factors as age, gender, climate, poverty, education and alcohol consumption. He collected data about many variables - an oft-quoted one being the chest measurements of Scottish soldiers – and was excited to find that they all followed a similar pattern.

This led on to his most influential book, *Treatise on Man*, published in 1835. In it, he described his concept of the 'average man', who is characterized by the mean values of measured variables, the range of each and every one of which could be represented by the a bell-shaped curve – otherwise known as the Gaussian or normal curve.

In passing, we should note that Quetelet also established a simple measure for classifying people's weight relative to an ideal weight for their height. His proposal, the body mass index (or Quetelet index), calculated as mass / height squared, has endured with minor variations to the present day.

Ranges

Francis Galton was fascinated by ranges, and developed the concept of the median, i.e. the middle point of the range when listed in order. It is important to register the fact that this is not the same as what is usually referred to as the average, i.e. the arithmetic mean (the aggregate value divided by the number of items). If you list the incomes or wealth of people in the U.K. in ascending order, for example, the median is significantly lower than the arithmetic mean – a fact that has serious political implications.

Galton went on to highlight the upper and lower quartiles, respectively 25% and 75% of the way through the range when listed in order, and introduced the idea of the '5 number summary' (top and bottom, upper and lower quartiles and median) to describe a range – which is still in use today.

He was also instrumental in measuring dispersion, in the form of the 'standard deviation' (the square root of the average of the squares of the individual deviations from the arithmetic mean). Again, this helped to describe and compare ranges, e.g. though they might have the same average temperature, a coastal city will show a lower dispersion than an inland one, on account of the mitigating effect of the sea.

Putting this into the context of the normal curve, he showed how 95% of the values will lie within two standard deviations of the mean, an observation that is fundamental to the interpretation of data collected on a sample basis. Crucially, he developed the idea of the Normal Probability Plot, which demonstrates how closely a data set resembles what would be expected on the basis of chance (i.e. the normal distribution).

Correlation

Francis Galton was also interested in comparing sets of data. We saw in chapter 1 how he had noted that people who possessed a particular attribute often had a parent who possessed it. To further his understanding of heredity, he wanted to quantify the similarity, and this led him to develop the concepts of correlation and regression.

Two variables are said to correlate if a change in one of them is accompanied by a change in the other, but Galton wanted to demonstrate just how closely one variable tracked the other. His solution took the form of the concept of the 'coefficient of correlation' which could be anything between +1 and -1:

- at one extreme, a coefficient of + 1 meant a perfect, direct, fit:

- at the other, a coefficient of – 1 meant a perfect but inverse fit;

- meanwhile, a coefficient of 0 meant no correlation at all;

- but most observations will be somewhere in between.

A modern day example is when the achievements of children in secondary schools are compared with their achievements in primary school – and reasons sought where the two are not closely correlated. One of Galton's innovations was to develop the technique so as to be able to apply it to examples involving different units. This facilitated an advance on the work of his father, noted in chapter 1, in drawing attention to (but not quantifying) what he had called 'parallelism': of prices, the money supply and the exchange rate.

The mathematics of correlation were taken much further by Karl Pearson but, until the advent of the computer, involved substantial calculations. These days, it is a function within Microsoft Excel, providing immediate quantification.

Regression

In 1877, in a lecture to the Royal Institution, Galton reported on experiments with sweet peas (which he had undertaken without knowing that Mendel was also doing so, in his work on genes). Galton had observed that, where the size of a seed was above the median of a batch, the seed of its offspring would also be above the median of its batch – but by a lesser degree. Similarly, where the size of a seed was below the median of a batch, the seed of its offspring would also be below the median of its batch – but by a lesser degree. As the generations progressed, therefore, the sizes of all seeds tended towards the median. This prompted Galton to coin the expression 'regression towards mediocrity'.

In 1884, he set up an 'anthropometric laboratory' at the International Health Exhibition in London. He took 15 measurements in respect of each of around 10,000 visitors – the results of which, he found, fitted the normal curve. The visitors included many pairs of parents and children, and he discovered that children's measurements – as with sweet peas – were closer to their median than their parents' measurements were to theirs.

Putting these ideas together, he invented a way of expressing relationships, i.e. the amount of change in one variable for a given change in the other. In this case, given the height of parents, relative to the mean, he could calculate the probable height their offspring relative to its median. In that particular case, the 'regression' ratio was 2 / 3, e.g. a child with a mid-parental height 3 inches taller than median can be 'statistically expected' to be (i.e. will most probably be) only 2 inches taller than median for its age group.

Though not exactly what Galton intended, people began to use the word 'regression' to describe any formula which shows the relationship between two variables, which has found widespread use across the board, as an aid to forecasting and decision making.

In business, for example, the relationship between price and demand, and that between volume and cost can be expressed as formulae; putting them together helps the manager to see which price point will maximise profit. Such relationships also form the bedrock of financial modelling.

Recently, the expression 'big data' has come into the business lexicon, as massive computer power can be used to analyse large volumes of data, to see associations that are not obvious 'to the naked eye', such as between weather forecasts and sales volumes of particular products. Beware, however: correlation does not always signify cause and effect; sometimes it signifies two effects of a third cause, and occasionally mere coincidence, leaving room for considerable debate around any findings.

Applications

In his 1889 publication, *Natural Inheritance*, Galton commented that he found statistics 'full of beauty and interest. When delicately handled by the higher methods, and warily interpreted, their power of dealing with complicated phenomena is extraordinary'. He also explained his 'mechanical illustration of the curve of frequency' referred to earlier as the Quincunx. It was this book which was to attract the attention of Karl Pearson, who became his close associate and biographer.

An illuminating, if unusual, application of Galton's thinking was his 1872 paper *Statistical Enquires into the efficacy of prayer* in which reported that he had found no correlation between prayers and their consequences. Specifically, he had compared the lifespans of crowned heads of Europe (whose longevity was prayed for every week by large numbers of subjects) with their contemporaries. He built on this by asking such questions as the following.

- Why do insurance companies not distinguish between the pious and the profane?

- Why do doctors not prescribe prayer? This is an issue which has re-surfaced recently, in cases where nurses in the National Health Service have actually been forbidden to pray with patients.

- Why do churches install lightning conductors?

He did acknowledge, however, that prayer could provide personal, spiritual and psychological comfort and provide a communion with a transcendent universe. He rejected the idea of a God, but thought nature was worthy of worship.

Another variation on Galton's statistical work was described in an article he wrote for the 7th March 1907 edition of *Nature*. In it, he reported 'in these democratic days' on an investigation into 'the trustworthiness and peculiarities of popular judgements'. Specifically, he described a competition to guess the weight of an ox at the West of England Fat Stock and Poultry Exhibition in Plymouth. 800 tickets had been sold at sixpence a time, and prizes were awarded to those getting close to the actual weight. He commented that the average competitor was probably as well fitted for making a just estimate of the weight of the ox, as an average voter was of judging the merit of most political issues.

He recorded, arrayed and graphed the various entries, and found that, although there was a wide range, the median was accurate to within less than 1% (9 lbs in 1198) or, as he put it, 'the middlemost estimate expresses the *vox populi*'. Subsequent analysis showed that the arithmetic mean was accurate to within less than 0.1% (1 lb. in 1198). Galton's view is indicated by his interpretation that 'the result is more creditable to the trustworthiness of a democratic judgement than might have been expected'. Was this an endorsement of the idea of universal suffrage, which did not materialise until after his death?

The idea was revived in James Surowieki's 2004 book *The wisdom of crowds* in which he argued that a collection of individuals is likely to make certain kinds of decisions and predictions better than any one individual, however expert. The conditions required for this to be so are a diversity of opinion, independence, decentralisation and a means of aggregation. Examples are futures markets, consensus forecasting, and 'ask the audience'.

From the above, we see that Galton made massive contributions to statistics, not only as regards dispersion, correlation and regression, but in bringing them together to facilitate understanding of complex data. Important as they were in their own right, however, to the man himself their value was in providing evidence in support of his theories of heredity, to which we now turn.

4. Heredity and psychology

Hereditary Character and Talent

It was, and remains, generally recognised that physical traits, such as height and colouring, are 'passed on' from one generation to the next. The conventional wisdom in Galton's day, however, was that mental characteristics, such as talents and temperaments – be they positive (such as intelligence) or negative (such as alcoholism) - were acquired, not inherited.

Galton's first publication on the subject, namely *Hereditary Character and Talent,* was a twenty-page article published in two parts, in *Macmillan's Magazine* in November 1864 and April 1865. In it, he declared his aim as being to demonstrate that mental characteristics were also under hereditary control 'on account of conditions we don't understand' (as noted earlier, he was unaware, at that time, of Mendel's work on genes – see below).

He referred back to his observations at Cambridge, and asserted that mental resemblances within families were too common to be the result of chance. Drawing on various surveys, he applied his concepts of correlation so as to quantify the extent to which eminence (in science, the arts, the law and the military) was hereditary.

Between 1866 and 1868, Galton's own mental health problems returned, and it was 1869 before he published a follow-up, called *Hereditary Genius – an inquiry into its laws and consequences.* In it, he said that his aim was 'to show that a man's natural abilities are derived from inheritance, under exactly the same limitations as are the form and physical features of the whole organic world'. He pointed out that human beings varied in mental abilities no less than in physical endowments, and said that he had no patience with the hypothesis that babies are born pretty much alike and that differences were the result of application and effort.

Acknowledging the work of Quetelet on applying the law of frequency of error to human physique, he looked at a wide variety of English families, around 300 in all, in occupations from artists through judges to scientists. They did show that mental characteristics followed a similar pattern, fitting the normal curve. He categorised men in seven classes expressed in terms of rarity: 1 in 4 for grade A, rising to 1 in 79,000 for grade G, recognising three attributes: intellectual capacity, eagerness to work, and power of working.

Englishmen of Science

In 1874, he published *Englishmen of Science: their nature and nurture*, based on replies to his 1870 questionnaire (the world's first, another of his innovations) to members of the Royal Society. It is on the basis of this title that he is sometimes credited with inventing the juxtaposition of nature and nurture but, in fact, Shakespeare had used it in *The Tempest*, with Prospero saying of Caliban, 'A devil, born devil, on whose nature nurture can never stick' (Act IV, Scene I, lines 211-212). Overall, *The Tempest* is markedly opposed to the idea that nature must be made 'civilized', indicating that a wild, natural world is superior to a culturally advanced one.

Galton's view on nature versus nurture contradicted the philosophies propounded by people like John Locke and John Stuart Mill, who had positioned the human mind as a 'blank slate', inscribed by experience. The debate is usually characterised as a contrast between two extremes:

- if your father was a good mathematician, you will be so too; or

- anyone can be a good mathematician given the right tuition and hard work.

Galton's view, however, was different, namely that if your father was a good mathematician, the *probability* that you will be a good mathematician is above average. Given a similar set of circumstances, people will still vary from one another, because they have different hereditary backgrounds. He therefore saw nurture as an enabling force, rather than a creative one, but important if innate qualities were to find the fullness of expression. Eminence, he asserted, could not be acquired – but would come to the surface. Galton stressed that he did not dismiss the benefits of nurture, but felt that nature was far more important.

In 1875 he published *The history of twins* which re-emphasised the nature v. nurture point. As a rule, he reported, he had found that identical twins remain similar even if separated, and that non-identical twins remain dissimilar even though reared together, findings which supported the argument that nature prevails over nurture.

The nature v nurture debate rumbles on to this day, as evidenced by a number of reports of which we might highlight the following.

- One issued in May 2012, on a study of over 800 pairs of twins, by a team led by Professor Timothy Bates of Edinburgh University. The study found that identical twins were twice as likely, as non-identical twins, to share various traits seen as important in determining success in life, such as: determination to overcome challenges; self-control; social skills; capacity to learn; a sense of purpose; and decision making ability. Professor Bates was quoted as saying that 'Previously, the role of the family and the environment around the home often dominated people's ideas about what affected psychological

38

well-being. However, this work highlights a much more powerful influence from genetics.' This is just one example of how Galton's work seems to have been lost thanks to the revisionism of the post-war years.

- In 2013, a study of GCSE results, led by Prof Robert Plomin of the Institute of Psychiatry at King's College London, concluded that genetics accounted for twice as much of a person's intelligence as environmental factors. Interestingly, that ratio tends to increase as people age (probably a polarisation thing: brighter children read more, and mix with brighter children). He argued that the educational establishment had been too quick to dismiss the influence of genetics for fear of 'labelling' children. They should focus, he said, on tailoring education to individual needs, rather than delivering it on a one-size-fits-all basis. Other studies have shown that equality of nurture actually increases differences in achievement as between superior and inferior (because the former are keener to grasp the opportunities).

- The popular media noted that, in the second test match between England and New Zealand, in May 2013, 5 of the 22 players were sons of test cricketers and one was the grandson of a test cricketer. Does this provide evidence of the importance of nature (innate skill) rather than nurture (encouragement and guidance) or a combination of the two? A writer in the *Daily Telegraph* mused on the unfair advantage that would accrue to the children of Andre Agassi and Steffi Graf should they take up tennis!

Natural Inheritance

Writing in the journal of the Anthropological Institute in 1886, Galton recalled his findings on *Regression towards mediocrity*, and reported on work on a large number of family records. He had found that the more gifted a parent is, the more exceptional is the good fortune of a parent whose child equals or surpasses him in that respect. At the same time, however, he insisted that his findings did not invalidate 'the general doctrine that the children of a gifted pair are much more likely to be gifted than the children of a mediocre pair'.

The conventional wisdom at the time was that all traits were *blended* as generation followed generation. Neither Darwin nor Galton were able to identify the mechanism of heredity and were therefore puzzled by its inconsistency – though the latter suspected that there was a probability aspect to it. Having disproved (by transfusion) an early hypothesis that the blood was the carrier, Galton concluded that it came from the sperm and egg, and therefore could not be changed during one's lifetime.

Beyond that, it would remain a mystery until the rediscovery of the work of **Gregor (born Johann) Mendel 1822 – 1884,** an Augustinian friar, based in what is now the Czech Republic, and founder of the Austrian Meteorological Society. He developed an interest in the variation in plants, specifically peas, where he focused on seven character traits in peas: purple or white flowers; round or angular seeds; white or grey seed coatings; smooth or bumpy pod; green or yellow young pod; flowers on tip or stem; tall or short.

He found that these fundamental traits were passed on by way of *discrete units,* and went on to describe the patterns in reproduction, i.e. the laws of inheritance, in mathematical terms, and presented his findings in his 1865 paper *Experiments in plant hybridisation.* Specifically, he showed that, for each trait, there was a dominant factor and a recessive factor. He went on to show that these are paired randomly in three different ways: D+D, R+R and D+R. Echoing what we noted as regards the toss of two coins, the last mentioned occurs twice as often as each of the other two, hence the dominant factor will determine the character three times as often as the recessive one – ushering in the opportunity to apply the laws of probability.

Let us take the everyday example of hair colour, and consider the children born to a couple, one of whom has only the gene for brown hair (which is dominant) and the other only the gene for red hair (which is recessive). All will have brown hair, but each will have one 'brown' gene and one 'red' one. If those children, in turn, have children with someone with a similar combination (i.e. brown hair but carrying a dormant 'red' gene) the probabilities as regards their children's hair colour are as follows:

- 1 in 4 will have red hair and will pass on only red genes;
- 2 in 4 will have brown hair but will, like their parents, pass on a red gene as well as a brown one;
- 1 in 4 will have brown hair and will pass on only a brown gene.

For some reason Mendel's work had little impact at the time. In 1900, however, independent research by Hugo de Vries and Carl Correns led to the re-discovery of Mendel's work, and to the establishment of the science of genetics.

Education

Galton's view was that heredity was the main determinant of success and, in the first half of the nineteenth century, only very well-off parents could afford to pay for the formal education of their children. It was a case of something like 5% of the population getting 95% of the formal education that was available. This would have seemed quite normal at the time, and we should also bear in mind that:

- the prevailing mood in the country was one of *laissez faire*, which did not welcome government intervention;

- the upper classes had no wish to see the general population better educated, not least on account of the fear of revolution such as had occurred in France (a significant stamp duty was levied on newspapers until 1855);

- the working classes had no wish to lose the income earned by their children should they sacrifice work for education.

Society was polarised, in the sense that children of rich families tended to meet one another, marry, and raise children who would enjoy the same benefits, thereby keeping wealth, power – and probably eminence - within the family.

By the second half of the century, however, alongside parliamentary reform, the mood was changing towards a more collectivist one, and it was noted that the country was becoming uncompetitive against others which had better-educated work forces. In particular, the new factories needed workers who could read, count and measure. Two societies were formed in 1865 – the Education League and the National Education Union - which were very influential in bringing about legislation to expand education, as follows.

- In 1870, school boards were established and authorised to render attendance compulsory;

- From 1876 onwards, parents failing to secure education for their children could be punished;

- In 1880, school boards were obliged to render attendance compulsory;

- and, by 1891, what we now term *primary* education was compulsory and free of charge. This meant that the poor could not send their children out to work, which may have prompted them to have fewer. There is no doubt that literacy improved dramatically, opening the way for emergence of popular newspapers, led in 1896 by the *Daily Mail*.

Significant change in the secondary sector, however, would have to wait until the end of the Second World War, as we shall see in chapter 10.

Psychology

Arising out of his study of heredity, Francis Galton was also responsible for a number of innovations in psychology, notably the following.

- Word association tests, and their relevance to 'deeper strata of mental operations, sunk wholly below the level of consciousness', an idea that was picked up by Freud and other psychoanalysts dealing with the unconscious mind. Galton saw the speed of response as an indicator of intelligence.

- Tests of cognitive ability (the capacity to perform higher mental processes of reasoning, remembering, understanding, and problem solving).

- Psychometry, i.e. the quantification of mental faculties, making the observation in *Brain* in 1879 that until the phenomena of any branch of learning have been subjected to measurement and number, it cannot assume the status and dignity of a science. These days, the principles can be seen in operation in Belbin's 'team chemistry' work, the Myers-Briggs 'type indicators', and various aptitude tests used in schools and by employers.

- The founding of the specialist discipline of differential psychology. Edinburgh University claims to have the world's largest group dedicated to this area today, using 'individual differences in behaviour as a window onto psychological mechanisms including the genetic and environmental origins of individual differences in intelligence and personality'.

- Visual imagery, as regards which he drew attention to differences between:

    a) the sexes (the power of visualising being higher among women than men);

    b) ages (the power declining as we get older); and

    c) races (the Eskimos being able to visualise vast tracts of country).

- Various sensitivity tests, including one for hearing, using a variable whistle, which identified the frequency up to which people could hear (the older you are, the lower that point) and which is still in use – and known as the Galton whistle, or the dog whistle.

However, we now need to turn to the most controversial product of his work on heredity, namely his concept of eugenics.

5. Galton's Eugenics

Forerunners

As with statistics, although much of Francis Galton's output was original, it is not difficult to identify influences from earlier writers, the following being worthy of particular note.

We know that Galton was reading Greek classics at an early age, and would have been aware of **Plato (426 – 347 BC)** who studied under Socrates, and established an academy which operated for 800 years, educating many great men, including Aristotle.

Plato rejected egalitarianism and democracy, and advocated rule by an elite, using personality, compulsion and violence. In his Socratic dialogue *The Republic*, written around 380 BC, he pointed out that livestock owners did not breed from all their animals indiscriminately, but only from those deemed to be the best. So it should be, he argued, with mankind. Specifically, he advised that, 'if the flock is to be as perfect as possible:

- the best men must cohabit with the best women in as many cases as possible, and the worst with the worst in the fewest;

- the offspring of the best must be reared and that of the other not, but the way this is brought to pass must not be known to any but the rulers;

- the offspring of the inferior, and any of the other sort who are defective, should be properly disposed of in secret.'

Rev Thomas Malthus (1766 – 1834) studied at Joseph Priestley's academy in Warrington, and at Cambridge University.

As a minister, he noticed that an increasing proportion of the children he baptised were poorly dressed and under-nourished.

In his *Essay on the Principles of Population*, the first edition of which was published in 1798, Malthus positioned poverty as divinely imposed to limit population growth (which would otherwise follow a geometric progression) to that which could be sustained. Rather than waiting for this to happen through famine, war or disease, however, he advocated preventative checks based on a foresight of the difficulties attending a family, and the fear of dependent poverty, specifically:

- moral restraint, whereby the poor are encouraged to delay getting married and having children;

- the gradual phasing out of the benefit system (the 'Poor Laws') which, he argued, created a debilitating dependency culture - an issue which resonates today.

Charles Darwin (1809 – 1882), as we have seen, was Galton's half-cousin. In his autobiography, he acknowledged that it was while reading the *Essay on the Principles of Population* that he first had the idea - that favourable variations tend to be preserved, and unfavourable ones destroyed – which underpinned his theory of evolution on the basis of natural selection. Darwin inspired Francis Galton by way of the various books which he wrote following his five year expedition (1831 – 6) notably:

- *On the origin of species* (1859)

- *The variation of animals and plants under domestication* (1866)

- *The descent of man, and selection in relation to sex* (1871)

46

His basic thesis (which advanced his grandfather Erasmus's ideas) was that new species were not created in each geological age, but were lineal descendants of earlier species. Thus all living and extinct species were related on a single genealogical family tree.

He recognised that the vast majority of living things did not survive to reproduce. The tiny minority that survived to perpetuate their kind had made it through a competitive struggle for existence – for food, mates, living space, etc. - while the worst stock was cut off before it had chance to reproduce. He described this process as one of the natural selection of those best fitted for the prevailing environment.

Incidentally, the expression 'survival of the fittest' was not Darwin's. It was first used by **Herbert Spencer (1820 – 1903)** in his *Principles of Biology* published in 1864. Note the reciprocal definition in all of this, however: fitness was defined in terms of relative reproductive success; traits become more common if they aid success in reproduction. Spencer was a eugenicist before the term was coined, as evidenced by his assertion that 'The ultimate result of shielding men from folly is to fill the world with fools'.

From the outset, Darwin's explanation of evolution was characterised by controversy, mainly because of the inference that human beings were descended from animals, which was seen as an attack on the role of a creator, the Abrahamic God as described in the book of Genesis. In passing, it is worth noting that Darwin saw the differences between human races as too superficial to class them as separate species, and was fiercely opposed to slavery.

The conventional theological belief at the time was that nature had to preserve the same order and harmony as had reigned in the Garden of Eden; hybridisation was unnatural. They believed that the earth is only 6,000 years old, that different species had been separately created, and that fossils are not the remains of ancient organisms, but were placed there in their present form by God.

Some participants in the debate accepted evolution, but balked at natural selection, believing that divine intervention was necessary. Others believed that the creator had made the first living forms, with the capacity to evolve. The most well documented debate was that in Oxford, between the self-styled 'Darwin's bulldog', Thomas Huxley (supporting evolution) and Bishop Samuel Wilberforce (opposing).

Support for 'creationism' is still strong today, with some educational establishments insisting on 'teaching what the leaders believe, rather than some theory' (i.e. evolution).

Meanwhile, the general idea spread to other disciplines such as laissez faire economics and the free competitive market. In this guise, it was linked to the work of **Adam Smith (1723 – 1790),** a Scottish philosopher and an economist who had collaborated with David Hume on many projects. His main works were *The theory of moral sentiments* (1759) and *An enquiry into the nature and causes of the wealth of nations* (1776).

In particular, he is best remembered for having used the expression 'the invisible hand' to explain the power of the market economy, in which the pursuit of self-interest maximises the aggregate wealth of the community. He actually put it more colloquially: 'It is not from the benevolence of the butcher and baker that we expect our dinner, but from their regard for their own self-interest'. He wrote about the benefits of the division of labour but, significantly, warned of the dangers of collusion amongst producers, and of the likely wide disparities in income and wealth.

Hereditary Character and Talent, 1865

Galton's first comments of a eugenic nature (although he was not to coin the word until 1883) appeared in this publication as, echoing Plato, he commented as follows.

'How vastly would the offspring be improved, supposing distinguished women to be married to distinguished men.' This led him to muse on the idea of an annual competition to find the most eminent of the year's 25 year old men and 21 year old women, and to reward them with a dowry enabling them to marry (and procreate) earlier than they otherwise would.

'If a twentieth part of the cost were spent on measures for the improvement of the human race that is spent on the improvement of the breed of horses and cattle, what a galaxy of genius might we not create'.

He took the opportunity of citing examples where ignoring the significance of inheritance led to sub-optimisation - criticising the Roman Catholic Church, for example, for having attracted men of genius to be priests, and then insisted on their celibacy.

His main message was that, if the importance of heredity was recognised, then a programme could be put in place whereby the eminent were encouraged to marry and procreate, and the 'refuse' discouraged. He saw this as a gradualist approach, in that 'it would be quite practicable to produce a highly gifted race of men by judicious marriages during several successive generations'.

Interestingly, the evidence he collected did not support the theory put forward by Jean-Baptiste Lamarck (1744 – 1829), namely that *acquired* characteristics were passed on, prompting Galton to hypothesise that, rather, all the passing on was 'from embryo to embryo'. Or, as Richard Dawkins was to say much later 'The chicken is only the egg's way for making another egg'.

In Galton's view, culture and technology had developed, and branches of knowledge extended, to the point that 'few people are capable of comprehending the exigencies of modern civilisation, much less of fulfilling them'. He called for intervention to enable biological development to catch up, but noted that 'the general intellectual capacity of our leaders needs to be raised'.

There were also racial elements in the *Hereditary Character* article, such as the view that 'feeble nations of the world are necessarily giving way to the nobler varieties of mankind'.

Darwin's reaction was summarised in his acknowledgement that: 'I do not think I ever in all my life read anything more interesting and original. You have made a convert of an opponent in one sense, for I have always maintained that, excepting fools, men did not differ much in intellect, only in zeal and hard work, and I still think this is an eminently important difference'.

Hereditary Genius, 1869

In this publication, Galton described his aim as being to show that 'a man's natural abilities are derived by inheritance under exactly the same limitations as are the form and physical features of the whole organic world'.

He went on to reiterate his conviction that the best way of producing 'a highly gifted race' would be to retard the average marrying age among the weak, and hasten it among the vigorous, but noted that:

- the influence of various social agencies had been strongly and banefully exerted in the precisely opposite direction, with the result that the strong were in danger of being crowded out by the weak;

- there was a strong tendency for the prudent part of mankind to be more likely to delay marriage (as they built their careers) and hence procreation than the imprudent.

- Again, at this point, he criticised the church and universities for having imposed celibacy on their chosen ones, and for persecuting intelligent free thinkers.

As well as looking at variations within a particular race, Galton included a chapter on 'the comparative worth of different races', focusing on the frequency with which races threw up men of high natural ability, whose work enriched civilisation. Here, he acknowledged that every long-established race has its peculiar fitness for the conditions under which it has lived, owing to the operation of Darwin's law of natural selection. However, he went on to argue that the more intelligent are more likely to prevail in the battle of life, and rated different races as follows:

- The Ancient Greeks were the highest calibre ever, two notches above Anglo Saxons, meaning that there was plenty of scope for the latter to progress (but he explained the decline of the Greeks in terms of increasingly lax morality, including marrying outside the race);

- Negroes were a couple of notches below Anglo Saxons, on the basis of their lack of cultural and industrial development;

- Australian aborigines were a further notch below Negroes.

He drew attention to the number of races of mankind that had been entirely destroyed under the pressure of the requirements of an incoming civilisation which, he said, provided 'a terrible lesson'. In particular, he suggested that in no former period of the world had the destruction of the races of any animal whatever been effected over such wide areas and with such startling rapidity as in the case of savage man.

Catholic World challenged Galton's findings and argued that, though he might be correct that all men are not born with equal natural abilities, the Church taught that they were born with equal natural rights.

In 1871, the topic received further publicity in Darwin's follow up book *The Descent of Man*, in which he followed Galton's thinking by comparing savages and civilised people. Amongst the former, he suggested, 'the weak in body or mind are soon eliminated; and those that survive commonly exhibit a vigorous state of health' whereas 'we civilised men do our utmost to check the process of elimination. Thus the weak members of civilised societies propagate their kind'. He was concerned to observe that 'the reckless, degraded and often vicious members of society tend to increase at a quicker rate than the provident and generally virtuous members'.

Meanwhile, he saw the Europeans as 'having so immeasurably surpassed their savage progenitors that they stand at the summit of civilisation'.

Galton's views on race were taken further in June 1873, in a letter he wrote to *The Times*, entitled 'Africa for the Chinese' urging on the government a policy under which Chinese people would be encouraged to settle in Africa. He went on to argue that:

- they would not only maintain their position but would multiply, and their descendants would supplant the inferior Negro race. Large areas then occupied by lazy, palavering savages might, in a few years, be tenanted by industrious, order-loving Chinese;

- there had been instances of Negroes possessing high intelligence and culture, but these had been the exception. Negroes generally possessed too little intellect, self-reliance and self-control to make it possible for them to sustain any respectable form of civilisation;

- the Chinaman was a being of another kind, with a remarkable aptitude for a high material civilisation. There was none so appropriate as the Chinaman to become the future occupant of the enormous regions which lie between the tropics whose extent, he observed, 'is far more vast than it appears from the cramped manner in which the latitudes are pictured in the ordinary maps of the world.'

This was prophetic in a way, in that the twenty-first century is seeing massive investment in Africa by the Chinese, anxious to protect supplies of key materials.

Hereditary Improvement, 1873

The next milestone came with the publication, in Fraser's magazine, of an article entitled *Hereditary Improvement*, in which Galton gave his reaction to criticism that, though the idea that character was strongly influenced by heredity was by then widely accepted, it could never be of practical benefit, because men and women would continue to marry according to their personal likings. Specifically, he kicked off the hobby of genealogy, by proposing a gradual process as follows.

'The English race should be explored, and those who are naturally gifted should be identified, and recorded on a national register. Families should be encouraged to record details of health, strength, intellectual capacity, character weaknesses etc., with as much narrative as possible.' He saw a benefit in this in that people would be warned against marrying / having children with those likely to pass on such disorders. In practice, however, families saw mental illness as a stain on the character of the entire family, and were prompted to hush up any such problems. In turn, this drove the development of asylums where the mentally ill would be locked away. (As noted in chapter 1, Great Barr Hall, the family home of Galton's grandfather Samuel, and favourite meeting place of the Lunar Society, was to become Barr Colony, housing 'imbeciles, idiots and the feeble minded'.)

Social favour and preference should be procured for the gifted ones. He noted that, just as Queen Elizabeth I had 'given promotion to well-made men', future landowners might take pride in being 'surrounded by magnificent specimens.'

It was reasonable to expect that these gifted people would, with the encouragement of dowries, intermarry at an early age, and thereby have more children than they otherwise might. They should not squander their patrimony, he argued, by marrying out of their caste. He saw the dowries being managed by the state, and at least partly funded by a limitation on the freedom to bequeath wealth (which he saw as interfering with the 'salutary action of natural selection').

As time went by, he predicted, eminent people would coalesce, with the force almost of a religion. They would separate themselves from the rest, and establish their own institutions, such as building societies, insurance schemes etc. Therein, the new higher form of civilisation would evolve. If persecuted, they should emigrate and become the parents of a new state with a glowing future [the basic idea in Aldous Huxley's *Brave New World*].

Along the way, he lamented the absence of civilisations which are co-operative, in which the good of the community was a more vivid desire than self-aggrandisement. It should be seen as the religious duty of intelligent men, he asserted, to advance in the direction whither nature determines they should go, i.e. to render their individual aims subordinate to those which lead to the improvement of the race. Breeding out the feeble, and breeding in the vigorous, should be a passion. In support of his assertion, he drew attention to nature in the wild, in which the life of the individual is of no importance, the species is everything.

In that context, he echoed Malthus, saying that he deplored charitable actions which have a notorious tendency to demoralise the recipient, and to increase the extent of the very evils to which they were a response. One exception might be assistance conditional upon celibacy of the recipient; otherwise, they should face 'the ominous consequences of being seen as enemies of the state'. He acknowledged that his ideas would appear to conflict with the growing feeling for democracy, but felt that people would, eventually:

• recognise that the doctrines of heredity are true;

• recognise and respect eminence;

• see the perpetuation of the stronger / wiser / more moral as being the obvious intention of nature.

Either way, however, he concluded that, if democracy asserts that all men are of equal value as social units, then it is undeniably wrong. To put this in context, we might note that, during Galton's lifetime, the electoral franchise was steadily broadened – by:

a) The 1832 Great Reform Act, promoted by Lord John Russell when leader of the Whigs, which abolished rotten boroughs (those with only a handful of voters) and introduced representation to urban centres such as Birmingham (which had previously had none). It aimed to ensure that votes had equal weight across the various constituencies but, over time, this has drifted.

b) The Reform Acts of 1867 and 1884 – to cover all males over 25 who owned their homes. As late as the year of Galton's death (1911), however, Members of Parliament were not paid either salary or expenses; they were a group of part-timers, most of them quite rich. Notwithstanding that, the Labour Party had by then come into existence, sponsored by the Trade Union movement, and was gaining ground rapidly.

Support for Galton's ideas was widespread, a typical view being that expressed in an article by respected historian George William Rusden (1819 – 1903) in the Melbourne Review in 1876, in which he asserted that:

• the concept of the survival of the fittest means that might, wisely used, was right;

• it was the inexorable law of natural selection that had led to the extermination of Australia's aborigines.

An interesting development, around this time, was the appearance of Anthony Trollope's *The fixed period*. Published in 1882, the year he died aged 67, it told a story, set a hundred years into the future, on an island republic that had enacted a law which required people reaching the age of 67 to submit to euthanasia. The book rehearsed the case for such a policy, e.g. relieving the individual of misery, and the community of the cost of care. However, it concluded that, though it would improve society as a whole, the personal impact was such that no-one would ever be willing to put it into practice. He could not have anticipated Nazi policies.

Inquiries into human faculty 1883

It was in this book, that Galton used the term 'eugenics' for the first time, defining it as 'the scientific study of the biological and social factors which improve or impair the inborn qualities of human beings and of future generations.' Elaborating, he emphasised that it was not confined to questions of judicious mating, but took cognisance of 'all influences that tend to give the more suitable races a better chance of prevailing speedily over the less suitable, than they otherwise would'. He suggested, in another echo of Malthus, that there was a need to 'consider whether it might not be our duty to improve the human stock by such efforts as may be reasonable, thus exerting ourselves to further the ends of evolution more rapidly and with less distress than if events were left to their own course'.

He went on to suggest that:

- the life of an individual is, in some real sense, a prolongation of those of his ancestry;

- the whole of the living world moves steadily and continually towards the evolution of races that are progressively more adapted to their complicated mutual needs, and to their external environment;

- the process of evolution has been hitherto carried out with great waste of opportunity and of life;

- man ought to begin to assume a deliberate part in furthering the great work of evolution, making progress less painful.

Having paid 'humble tribute' to the work of Thomas Malthus, Galton emphasised that an imposed *general* deferral of marriage / procreation would be inappropriate, because it would be followed

57

only by the better people, i.e. the prudent and self-denying; the impulsive and self-seeking would ignore it. Fertility was inversely correlated with the woman's age: hence the better should marry earlier (encouraged by dowries, etc.) thereby improving the stock – but, in fact, they tended to delay marriage until their careers were firmly established.

In an echo of Adam Smith's 'invisible hand', he noted that individuals are, for the most part, unconscious of the fact that, while working for themselves, they are working for the common good.

He devoted a section to discussing the identification of the better stock, under two headings:

- personal traits, like health, morality, energy, intelligence, industriousness and fair-mindedness;

- ancestral, evidenced by achievements, linked to longevity and stamina.

In conclusion, he expressed the view that man should use his intelligence to discover and expedite the changes that are necessary to adapt circumstance to race, and race to circumstance – and that 'his kindly sympathy will urge him to effect them mercifully'.

Scientific archaeology

Around this time, Galton developed a friendship with **Sir (William Matthew) Flinders Petrie 1853 – 1942**, who was regarded as 'the father of scientific archaeology, with a special interest in Egypt, and was himself a member of an eminent family, his maternal grandfather being Matthew Flinders (1774 – 1814), the first person to circumnavigate Australia, in 1802, and recognise that it was a continent.

In 1883, the Royal Society was about to offer a grant to survey / measure the pyramids. On hearing of this, Petrie drew their attention to the fact that he had done just that over the previous two years. The Society asked Francis Galton to review his work – which he did, and, was able to report favourably, recommending that the Society pay for publication.

This was the beginning of a productive association between the two men. In 1886, with funding from the British Association for the Advancement of Science, Galton hired Petrie to return to Egypt and to photograph ancient portraits and death masks of different racial types. The results were published in *Racial Photography* in 1887.

Thereafter collaboration continued, with Petrie sending thousands of skeletons, skulls and other bones for Galton to measure and classify, and corresponding on various matters of statistics, heredity, anthropometrics and eugenics. This collaboration clearly influenced Petrie in his work on civilisation, race and culture, and encouraged him to think in terms of improving the human race. He was appointed the country's first ever Professor of Egyptology (at University College London, thanks to a bequest by Amelia Edwards, and where today's Petrie Museum houses many of his finds). He supported the logic of Darwin's evolution but went further by encouraging individuals to participate in social change through artificial selection, i.e. choosing the best mates.

He went on to publish two important books:

- *Janus in modern life* (1907) in which he stressed the need to look both backwards and forwards in order to be alert to evils to come. He rejected social welfare and the redistribution of wealth on the grounds that that it allowed those who were uncompetitive to remain so. He reminded readers of the gospel message of giving to him that hath, and taking from him that hath not. He advocated promoting the most vigorous strains, and sterilising the worst.

- *The revolution of civilisation* (1911) in which he argued that the harder a nation strives, the more capable it will be. Diversity and competition were to be fostered, but equality was inappropriate as it discouraged striving. On a larger scale, fine races needed to be segregated.

Hereditary Genius again

In 1892, *Hereditary Genius* was reprinted, with an additional preface in which Galton noted that, at the time of the original publication, the conventional wisdom was that the human mind was 'capable of almost any achievement if compelled to exert itself by a will that had a power of initiation'. He also explained that the title had been based on Dr Johnson's definition of genius - an exceptionally high, and inborn, ability – but that, as usage had developed, a better title would be *Hereditary Ability.*

Somewhat ominously, in view of subsequent developments, he floated the idea that the time might have arrived when an institute for experiments on heredity might be established with advantage.

He identified a direct result of his inquiries as being the observation that the rules of heredity were as applicable to mental characteristics as to physical ones – and an indirect one as being to show that a vast power is vested in each generation over the very natures of their successors. It was here that he explained his finding that there was a regression to the median as generation followed generation, but that there remained in every generation 'a typical centre, from which individual variations occur, in accordance with the law of frequency' (i.e. the normal curve).

He pointed to the need to consider the relative fertility of different classes and races, and their tendency to replace one another under various circumstances. Again chiming with the views of the Reverend Malthus, he challenged the idea that there is no limit to population other than misery or prudential restraint. Rather, he argued, 'Man is gifted with pity and other kindly feelings, and has the power of preventing many kinds of suffering. I conceive it well within his province to replace natural selection by other processes that are more merciful and not less effective'.

On a broader canvas, he expressed the view that 'The frequency in history with which one race has supplanted another over wide geographical areas is one of the most striking facts in the evolution of mankind.'

In 1901, Galton addressed the Royal Anthropological Society on the practicalities of improving the race and, in 1904, he established the first chair of eugenics, at University College London (which led on to the setting up of the Galton Laboratory in 1907). The first holder of the chair was **Karl Pearson 1857 – 1936,** who is seen as the founder of mathematical statistics. Karl was born Carl but changed his name, out of admiration for all things German. He worked with Francis Galton in the last few years of the latter's life, and wrote his definitive biography. He described his view of a nation as 'that of an organised whole, kept up to a high pitch of internal efficiency by ensuring that its numbers are substantially recruited from the better stock, and kept up to a pitch of external efficiency by contest, chiefly by way of war with inferior races'. [Ian Morris's *War, what is it good for?* published in 2014 seems to support this idea.]

Speaking at a Social Society meeting in London in 1904, Galton urged persistence in setting forth the national importance of eugenics, suggesting that there were three stages to be passed through:

- It must be made familiar as an academic question, until its exact importance has been understood and accepted as a fact.

- It must be recognized as a subject whose practical development deserves serious consideration.

- It must be introduced into the national conscience, like a new religion. It has, indeed, strong claims to become an orthodox religion, a tenet of the future, given that eugenics seeks co-operation with the workings of nature by securing that humanity should be represented by the fittest races. What nature does blindly, slowly, and ruthlessly, man may do providently, quickly, and kindly. As it lies within his power, so it becomes his duty to work in that direction. The improvement of our stock seems to me one of the highest objects that we can reasonably attempt. We are ignorant of the ultimate destinies of humanity, but feel perfectly sure that it is as noble a work to raise its level, in the sense already explained, as it would be disgraceful to abase it.

Presciently, however, he warned that 'overzeal', leading to hasty action, would do harm, by holding out expectations of a near golden age, which would certainly be falsified and cause the science to be discredited.

The later years

In 1908 The Eugenics Education Society (now the Galton Institute) was founded. Galton explained that 'The first objective of eugenics is to check the birth rate of the unfit, instead of allowing them to come into being; the second is the improvement of the race by furthering the productivity of the fit, by early marriages and the healthful rearing of children.'

Galton's ideas were not really out of tune with prevailing mood. The period 1815 – 1914 is referred to by historians as Britain's Imperial Century, when 10 million square miles and 400 million people, were added to its empire. Its policies included the Pax Britannica, splendid isolation, and subjugation of other races. Think of the verdict on British imperial expansion uttered by Sir Wilfred Lawson MP in 1894: 'Formerly, we stole Africans from Africa, and latterly, Africa from the Africans'.

Think also of the hymn written in 1848 by Cecil Frances Alexander (1818 – 95) the wife of the Archbishop of Armagh, and renowned for *There is a green hill far away*, and *Once in Royal David's City*. She also wrote *All things bright and beautiful*, the third verse of which went as follows: The rich man in his castle, the poor man at his gate, God made them, high and lowly, and ordered their estate.

As time went by, however, people were increasingly uncomfortable with this – and in 1982 the ILEA banned the singing of this verse in London Schools.

As with Darwin, what opposition there was to eugenics came from those religious groups for whom all people are seen as equal in God's sight, and who see it as a duty to improve the lot of the disadvantaged. The parable of the seeds and weeds, where the master refused permission for the weeds to be pulled up (he would deal with them at the time of harvest) provided one basis for their view.

There was also a strong 'nurture' reaction, and Galton acknowledged that education would have a favourable short term impact, but only up to a limit defined by nature, and (echoing his dismissal of Lamarkism) with no chance of being passed on.

When Galton talked about some races being superior to others, he explained that he was drawing on the facts of evolution: how some races had supplanted others. The idea that all races were equal in this respect, he would have seen as ignoring the facts. This was something that would inevitably continue, prompting the question as to how the tribulations thereof could be alleviated by the studious exercise of prudence and enlightened foresight, so as to make the supplanting painless and humane.

Louisa died in 1897, after which Francis was accompanied and helped by his niece Eva Biggs. Ironically, Francis and Louisa had no children – or was this a conscious decision motivated by his vulnerability to nervous breakdowns?

If the story ended here, then Francis Galton would surely be recognised as having made enormous contributions across a wide spectrum of society. His writings on eugenics were benign, positive and innovative, looking to prevent problems and making a connection between biology and sociology. They were couched in long termist and considerate language, focusing on births (rather than deaths). He drew attention to a long running question, namely the relative importance of the individual here and now, and racial posterity.

So why has he been 'airbrushed' out of history? As we shall see in the next two chapters, the answer lies in the way in which other people adapted his eugenic ideas in a malign and negative way.

6. Fabians and fellow travellers

From right to left

I find the terminology of politics increasingly confused, as names are changed to create a different impression, or to catch a mood. Tony Blair's New Labour, for example, never used the word socialism, but it has since been revived. Similarly, today's Liberal Democrats have little in common with the Liberal Party of Victorian times. Moreover, oxymorons abound, as with 'progressive conservatives' and 'libertarian socialists'.

Perhaps the safest way to track developments is to go back to the idea of a spectrum and, for the avoidance of doubt, in this book I am thinking of:

- the left as leaning towards state control and preferring centralisation, public ownership, a planned economy, progressive taxes, equality, standardisation and monopoly, with the extreme case being totalitarianism;

- the right as leaning towards the freedom of the individual and preferring decentralisation, private ownership, a market economy, flat taxes, differentials, variety and competition, with the extreme case being anarchy.

Commentators often refer to the middle ground, or the political 'centre'. That might be a useful reference point at a moment in time, but it should be borne in mind that it moves over time. As we shall see in a chapter 8, since Galton's time there has been a consistently leftward movement.

The Fabians

Anyone coming to the subject of eugenics afresh is likely to be surprised to find that the early adapters of Galton's eugenics were all left of centre: 'progressives' who had strong faith in science, and central planning. They lauded the wisdom of the elite, and hence the ability of a few to decide the fate of the many. It was not a matter of what the people wanted, so much as what they *should* want, prompting the progressives to advocate social reform through government action, to mould the individual to the necessity of the group.

In the United Kingdom and Ireland, many of the early eugenicists were members of the Fabian Society, which was established in 1884 with the goal of a gradual implementation of socialism, and named after the Roman emperor Fabius Maximus, the Cunctator, who preferred wearing his enemies down, rather than engaging in pitched battles. His patient, cautious, delaying and elusive tactics during the early phases of the Second Punic War (218-201 BC) enabled the Roman army to regroup and defeat Hannibal's stronger Carthaginian army. The following members of the Society are of particular relevance to our study.

George Bernard Shaw 1856 – 1950, the Irish playwright, wrote most of the early Fabian pamphlets. He explained that the Fabians' goal was to be achieved by 'stealth, intrigue, subversion, and the deception of never calling Socialism by its right name.' He was a co-founder of the London School of Economics and *The New Statesman*, and a prolific writer on serious social topics but with an element of humour. He often wrote about the exploitation of the working class, but condemned democracy, on the grounds that the majority were too ignorant to vote intelligently. 'I have never had any feelings about the English working classes' he said, 'except a desire to abolish them and replace them by sensible people.'

Instead, he followed a philosophy derived from the ideas of Friedrich Nietzsche, (whom we shall meet in the next chapter), believing that the problem would eventually be corrected by the emergence of supermen with experience and intelligence to govern properly. In pursuit of this idea, in 1903, he published what some say was his most brilliant play: *Man and Superman*, in which the life force desires to make suitable marriages, to produce a purer and prouder race – with women being the choosers.

Shaw argued that fundamental socialism must embrace the socialisation of selective breeding. Moreover, at a meeting of the Eugenics Education Society in 1910, he advocated the use of a 'lethal chamber' and speculated on the possibility of developing 'a deadly but humane gas for the purpose of killing, many at a time, those unfit to live'.

Sydney Webb 1859 – 1947 (later Baron Passfield) was a Secretary of State in the Labour Government, and a co-founder of the London School of Economics and the *New Statesman*. Together with his wife Beatrice, he contributed to the development of trade unionism (in the process, coining the expression 'collective bargaining') and the co-operative movement.

He was the author of the infamous 'clause 4' of the Labour Party constitution which read: 'To secure for the workers by hand or by brain the full fruits of their industry and the most equitable distribution thereof that may be possible upon the basis of the common ownership of the means of production, distribution and exchange, and the best obtainable system of popular administration and control of each industry or service'.

That could have been interpreted in terms of co-operatives or municipalisation but, in practice, it was taken to mean nationalisation, and this remained the case until Tony Blair became leader of the Labour party in the mid nineteen nineties, and expunged the clause.

Webb introduced the term 'adverse selection' to indicate that society was going in exactly the opposite direction from that described by Darwin, which 'can hardly result in anything but national deterioration'. Beatrice, writing a minority view in the report on Eugenics and the Poor Law in 1909 argued that 'What we as eugenicists have got to do is to scrap the Old Poor Law, with its indiscriminate relief of the destitute as such, and replace it by an intelligent policy of so altering the social environment as to discourage or prevent the multiplication of those irrevocably below the National Minimum of Fitness.'

The Webbs supported the idea of a minimum wage on the grounds that that it would protect deserving workers from the undeserving by making it illegal to work for less. 'Unemployment of the unemployable' Sydney argued 'is a mark of social health. Of all the ways of dealing with these unfortunate parasites, the most ruinous to the country is to allow them to compete as wage earners'. His definition of the unfit covered 'criminals, the incorrigibly idle, and the morally deficient'. He observed in 1910 that 'no eugenicist can be laissez faire; he must interfere'.

H G Wells 1866 – 1946 studied under T H Huxley, at the Normal School of Science in Kensington (later the Royal School of Science, and now part of Imperial College). These days, he is probably most well known as an author of futuristic novels, within which he was able to express his hopes and fears for humanity. He foresaw aerial bombardment, chemical weapons, laser beams, genetic engineering and climate change. He was convinced that the world's problems could only be solved by way of global citizenship and government, but commented that, outside of Europe and the United States, he did not expect that any intelligence would be found which would be capable of grasping his plans.

He was one of a number of intellectuals who joined the International Brigade, fighting against Franco's 'Falange' Nationalists in the Spanish Civil War. This probably explains why his books were among those ceremonially burned by the Nazis, and why he was banned from visiting Fascist Italy.

He had his own slant on eugenics, commenting in the American Journal of Sociology in 1904 that 'I believe that now and always the conscious selection of the best for reproduction will be impossible and that to propose it is to display a fundamental misunderstanding of what individuality implies. It is in the sterilisation of failure, and not in the selection of successes for breeding, that the possibility of an improvement of the human stock lies'. He disagreed with the Catholic Church's opposition to birth control, but advocated an endowment scheme which paid mothers according to the progress of their children.

His novels often echoed eugenic thought, as in:

- *The Time Machine*, published in 1865, where he fantasised about the separation of the human race into two subspecies, the eloi and the morlocks;

- *Kipps, the story of a simple soul*, published in 1905, in which one of the characters refers to 'the extravagant swarm of new births' as being 'the essential disaster of the nineteenth century'.

Lord William Beveridge 1879 – 1963 was an economist and social reformer, whose academic career included spells as director of the LSE and as master of University College Oxford. Specialising in unemployment, he worked closely with the Webbs, and with Winston Churchill at the Board of Trade. He was a member of the Eugenics Society and, in 1909, he proposed that men who could not work should be supported by the state 'but with complete and permanent loss of all citizen rights – including not only the franchise, but civil freedom and fatherhood'. On another occasion, he warned of the danger of a 'stationary white population' leaving 'one race at the mercy of another's growing numbers.'

He is best known, however, for his 1942 report which served as the basis for the welfare state built by the post-war Labour government. He urged the government to fight the five giant evils: want, disease, ignorance, squalor and idleness. The antidotes were to be social insurance, the health service, education, housing policy and full employment. As the members of the House of Commons were debating his report, however, he was reassuring a meeting of the members of the Eugenics Society at the Mansion House that it was consistent with their views, being eugenic in intent and effect.

These two apparently contradictory strands may be reconciled in that

- he and likeminded people saw the welfare state as clearly identifying the less able, so that they could be segregated and discouraged from reproducing;
- the benefits were to be dependent on contributions, which favoured the industrious;
- as noted earlier, it was recognised by then that equality of opportunity magnifies inequality of outcome (the brighter being more alert to the benefits available).

The only contemporary intellectual I have identified as speaking out against eugenics is **G K Chesterton (1874 – 1936)**. In his view:

- along with evolution, eugenics was only a theory, an 'unfinished fantasy';

- progressivism was a ruse, designed to oppress the masses;

- there was a danger that the ideas would morph into something evil. 'Don't wait for the axe to fall' he urged, but 'stop it in the air'.

Fellow travellers

Others worthy of mention, in terms of developing the ideas along Fabian lines, were the following.

Leonard Darwin, 1850 – 1943, was the son of Charles Darwin, and was chairman of the Eugenics Society from Galton's death in 1911 until 1928. He was then made honorary president, a post which he held until his own death. He published two influential books: *The need for eugenics* (1926) and *What is eugenics?* (1928).

Montague Norman 1871 – 1950 was governor of the Bank of England from 1920 to 1944. He was instrumental in putting the United Kingdom back on the gold standard in 1925, which proved devastating to exports and hence industry. Along with Dr Schacht, Hitler's Economics Minister and president of the Reichsbank, he was a member of the Round Table, which provided finance to the Fabians. The two men were also key figures in the Bank for International Settlements which, in March 1939 (just days after Germany had invaded Czechoslovakia), instructed the Bank of England to transfer ownership of millions of pounds worth of gold from Czechoslovakia to Nazi Germany. This it did, and the gold was subsequently sold, to help finance German rearmament. Norman was a supporter of eugenics and, after the war, established the National Association for Mental Health.

Bertrand, third Earl, Russell (1872 - 1970). Writing in 'Icarus or the Future of science' in 1924, Bertrand Russell wrote that 'before long, birth control may become nearly universal among the white races; it will … diminish their numbers, at a time when uncivilised races are still prolific and are preserved from a high death rate by white science'. As regards encouraging the propagation of superior types, however, he warned of the dangers of prime ministers or bishops deciding which types were desirable. He urged the adoption of a scientific approach to society, in which the growth of population was limited, but felt that the only way this would come about was through a world government.

Sir Winston Churchill (1874 – 1965). In 1908, a Royal Commission recommended to the Liberal government that the compulsory detention of the inadequate, and the sterilisation of the unfit, were vital to the health of the wider society. Supporting the recommendations, Winston Churchill noted that the feeble minded deserved 'all that can be done for them by a Christian and scientific civilisation now that they are in the world' but that they should be 'segregated under proper conditions so that their curse dies with them and is not transmitted to future generations'.

A letter he wrote to the Prime Minister, H. H. Asquith, in 1910 included his view that: 'The unnatural and increasingly rapid growth of the Feeble-Minded and Insane classes, coupled as it is with a steady restriction among all the thrifty, energetic and superior stocks, constitutes a national and race danger which it is impossible to exaggerate. I am convinced that the multiplication of the Feeble-Minded, which is proceeding now at an artificial rate, unchecked by any of the old restraints of nature, and actually fostered by civilised conditions, is a terrible danger to the race'. He was a vice president of the Eugenics conference held in July 1912.

This was not an isolated view, as evidenced by a comment around that same time by Dean Inge of St. Pauls, namely that eugenics was so logical that it was 'opposed only by irrationalist prophets.'

The resulting Mental Deficiency Act of 1913 subdivided the mentally ill into four categories, namely (in order of increasing seriousness and likely lengths of confinement) the feeble minded, imbeciles, idiots and mental defectives. It rejected sterilisation but made it a punishable misdemeanour to marry a mental defective.

Asylums were designated 'colonies' with the purpose of separating defectives from the gene pool of the nation. Unmarried mothers were classed as 'morally and mentally defective' and therefore committed to asylums. The Act has been amended and adapted over the years, the latest Act being in 2007.

In an article written in 1920, Churchill identified two admirable subsets of the Jewish race: the nationalist Jews (patriotic citizens of the country in which they live) and the Zionist Jews (anxious to establish a homeland in Palestine). However, he also identified a third, 'absolutely disruptive' subset: the Internationalist Jews - 'leaders of a worldwide conspiracy for the overthrow of civilisation'.

Marie Stopes 1880 – 1958 had met Francis Galton at a meeting of the British Association for the Advancement of Science, had attended eugenics conferences, and had met Margaret Sanger (the American birth control pioneer) at a Fabian meeting. In 1918, Stopes published a manual on birth control, entitled *Wise*

Parenthood. Then, in 1921, she opened the London Mothers' Clinic, staffed by midwives and offering advice on contraception, and founded The Society for Constructive Birth Control and Racial Progress. She was in favour of sterilisation of the unfit, but strongly opposed to abortion. She took her ideas personally, to the point of disinheriting her son Harry (Stopes-Roe, 1924 -2014) for marrying a short sighted girl (Mary, daughter of the engineer famous for the bouncing bomb, Sir Barnes Wallis), choosing instead to leave a substantial sum to the Eugenics Society. Harry went on to obtain Bachelor's and Master's degrees in physics and a Doctorate in Philosophy, and became a leading light in the Humanist movement. He remained a loyal defender of his mother's work. Writing in *The Guardian* in 2008, for example, he argued that people who saw her as a 'notorious eugenicist and anti-Semite who advocated the sterilisation of poor women to promote the welfare of the race' were out of touch with the realities of the nineteen twenties, and stressed that she had acted out of a sense of duty to the less fortunate.

Lord John Maynard Keynes 1883 – 1946 is generally regarded as the founder of the theory and practice of macroeconomics and, as such, the most influential economist of the twentieth century. He won scholarships to Eton, and later to Cambridge, from which he graduated in mathematics and where he was later to lecture on economics. Amongst his most notable publications were the following.

• *The economic consequences of the peace*, which was published in 1919. In it, he described the Versailles Treaty at the end of the First World War as abhorrent and detestable insofar as it reduced Germany to servitude for a generation, degrading the lives of millions. He went on to predict that the reaction would lead to another war before which the horrors of 1914 - 18 would fade into nothing. The German hyperinflation of 1923, the collapse of the Weimar republic, the rise of Nazism and the Second World War proved him right.

- *The economic consequences of Mr Churchill*, which was published in 1925. In this, he exposed the depressing effect of the gold standard approach to managing the currency. The policy was abandoned but not until 1931.

- *The General Theory of Employment, Interest and Money*, his magnum opus, which was published in 1936. Here, he explained the case for counter-cyclical government intervention in the economy. He argued that demand is the key variable and advocated its stimulation in times of unemployment, e.g. by spending on public works. He was a passionate advocate of 'national self-sufficiency'.

He was a director of the Bank of England and chairman of the World Bank commission which established the Bretton Woods system of managed currencies – though he disagreed with the structure which put all the burden of correcting imbalances on deficit countries, on the grounds that they were the least able to address the problem – a situation reprised in the 21st century Eurozone.

He served as Director of the Eugenics Society from 1937 to 1944 and described eugenics as 'the most important, significant and genuine branch of sociology'. He favoured birth control on the grounds that the working class was too 'drunken and ignorant' to keep numbers down.

Sir Julian Huxley 1887 – 1975 was an evolutionary biologist, his outstanding work being *Evolution: the modern synthesis*. He was:

- the first director of the United Nations Educational, Scientific and Cultural Organisation ('UNESCO');

- one of the founders of the World Wildlife Fund, which set out to identify the causes of losses of charismatic species, and to devise ways of slowing such losses down and, if possible, stopping them;

- a prominent member of the Eugenics Society, being vice president 1937 – 1944 and president 1959 – 1962, and giving the Galton memorial lecture in both 1936 and 1962.

Reacting to Pope Pius XI's condemnation of sterilisation in 1930, he argued that 'in the long run, we must envisage the control of population in the same manner as we now control contagious disease.' Echoing Galton, he acknowledged that 'this may seem undemocratic but heredity and biology are not democratic'.

In 1939, he was one of the signatories of the Eugenics Manifesto, published in *Nature* and, in 1941, he wrote that 'the lowest strata are reproducing too fast. They must not have too easy access to relief and hospital treatment, lest the removal of the last checks on natural selection should make it too easy for children to be produced and to survive. Long term unemployment should be grounds for sterilisation.' On a more positive note, he put forward the idea of sperm banks, with eminent donors such as Nobel Prize winners.

As late as 1957, he was to write that society had to face up to the fact that the great majority of human beings were substandard: undernourished or ill, imprisoned in ignorance or superstition, and condemned to a ceaseless struggle for bare existence. He explained that he found himself driven to use the language of religion, in the sense of 'the relationship between man and his destiny'.

He was also to argue that unless society invents and enforces adequate measures for regulating human reproduction and, at least, preventing the deterioration of the quality of racial stock, they are doomed to decay.

J B S Haldane 1892 – 1964 was a Marxist biologist and geneticist, and one-time editor of *The Daily Worker*. In 1948, he said that 'In many countries, the poor breed quicker than the rich. Thus the valuable genes making for ability, which brings economic success, are getting rarer, and the average intelligence of the race is declining'. Writing in 1949, he explained that the dogma of human equality is no part of communism: if it were, he explained, the idea of 'from each according to his ability, to each according to his need' would be nonsense. He went on to applaud socially responsible eugenics, and acknowledge that races differed in the proportions of highly gifted people.

Aldous Huxley 1894 – 1963 was the grandson of 'Darwin's bulldog', Thomas Henry Huxley, and brother of Sir Julian (but Aldous himself turned down a proffered knighthood).

He worked for a while at Brunner Mond, one of the founding constituents of Imperial Chemical Industries, and described his experience as 'an ordered universe in a world of planless incoherence' and said it was one of the sources of his novel *Brave New World* (another expression borrowed from Shakespeare's *The Tempest*). In that book, the ideas of marriage and families were seen as laughable. Perhaps we are heading that way, given the incidence of divorce and unmarried pregnancies these days.

In January 1932, two weeks before its publication, in a BBC broadcast, he discussed the possible use of eugenics as an instrument of political control, and expressed his support for eugenic measures to arrest 'the rapid deterioration ... of the whole Western European stock'.

Around that time, to put such views into context, an article in the New Statesman argued that 'The legitimate claims of eugenics are not inherently incompatible with the outlook of the collectivist movement. On the contrary, they would be expected to find their most intransigent opponents amongst those who cling to the individualistic views of parenthood and family economics.'

Huxley had a morbid fascination with the economic muddle, political inertia and social unrest which shaped national life in the early 1930s. He disagreed with Keynes' view that the problem was one of under-consumption, to be solved by public works. Rather he favoured, at that time, the Russian '5 year plan' approach. In his 1946 update of *Brave New World*, however, his foreword made no reference to either planning or eugenics – this was, of course, after Hitler's reign - but suggested that the novel had foreseen the nightmarish future for communism.

As can be seen, eugenic thinking was fairly mainstream, but let us close this section with another quote from a religious authority. Delivering the Galton Lecture to the Eugenics Education Society in 1926, Ernest Barnes, then Bishop of Birmingham, concluded that 'When religious people realise that, in preventing the survival of the socially unfit, they are working in accordance with the plan by which God has brought humanity so far on its road, their objections to repressive action will vanish'.

The American bandwagon

Although the United States constitution declares that all men are created equal, for many years, the expression 'all men' was seen as referring only to whites. In 1903, Theodore Roosevelt warned that immigrants and minorities were too fertile, and that Anglo-Saxons risked committing "race suicide" by using birth control and failing to keep up 'baby for baby'. The severest of all condemnations should be that visited upon wilful sterility.

Indeed, that first decade of the twentieth century saw Galton's ideas being imported into the United States just as Gregor Mendel's principles of heredity were rediscovered. American eugenic advocates put the two together and concluded that the principles expounded by the latter explained the observations of the former, and positioned eugenics as a science. That period saw the establishment, with financial backing from wealthy foundations and individuals (notably the Carnegies, Rockefellers, Harrimans and Kelloggs) of such organisations as the American Breeders Association and the Eugenics Record Office (later Cold Spring Harbour Laboratory). Charles B Davenport was a leading activist and was later, with Eugen Fischer (yes, he of the Namibian atrocities), to establish the International Federation of Eugenics Organisations.

The American Breeders Association was formed specifically to 'investigate and report on heredity in the human race, and emphasise the value of superior blood, and the menace to society of inferior blood'. Alexander Graham Bell was an active member, having researched deafness (and advocated the prohibition of marriage of two deaf people) and also founded the Genealogical Record Office in Washington.

For many followers, sterilisation was considered a valid part of the solution to the menace of the feeble minded. By halting their reproductive capabilities, their traits would not be passed on to future generations. Compulsory sterilisation legislation was first introduced in Indiana in 1907, and was quickly adopted by other states. In 1922, The American Eugenics Society (later renamed The Society for the Study of Social Biology) was formed, again by wealthy industrialists and financiers, with the aim of 'stemming the tide of race degeneracy' promoted by way of lectures, books, etc. However, their approach differed from Galton's in that they argued that the state should prevent (rather than discourage) the unfit from procreating.

Even the United States Supreme Court supported aspects of eugenics. In the 1927 case of Buck v Bell, endorsing compulsory sterilisation, Supreme Court Justice Oliver Wendell Holmes wrote: 'It is better for all the world, if, instead of waiting to execute degenerate offspring for crime, or to let them starve for their imbecility, society can prevent those who are manifestly unfit from continuing their kind. Three generations of imbeciles are enough'.

By 1928, there were hundreds of curricula (involving over 20,000 students) that included eugenics, and the movement was very popular among women's clubs, especially in the South. One of the most prominent feminists to champion eugenics was Margaret Sanger, who had opened the first birth control clinic in 1913 (only to have it closed down by the police). Her objective was to prevent unwanted children from being born into a disadvantaged life, but she saw it as the individual women, rather than the state, who should make the key decision.

In her *Birth Control Review* in 1921, she wrote that 'the imbalance between birth rate of the unfit and fit is the greatest present menace to civilisation. The most urgent problem is how to limit and discourage over-fertility of the mentally and physically defective'. The following year, she established the Birth Control League (later renamed the Planned Parenthood Federation) and published *The pivot of civilisation* in which she argued that:

- 'uncontrolled fertility is universally correlated with disease, poverty and overcrowding;

- we are paying for .. the dictates of an ever increasing, unceasingly spawning class of human beings who should never have been born at all;

- we and our children must pay in one way or another for these biological and racial mistakes;

- birth control is thus the entering wedge for the eugenic educator;

- organised charity is a symptom of a malignant social disease - criticism is not directed at the failure of philanthropy but rather its success.'

A popular programme involved 'better baby' and 'fitter family' competitions and Christian churches – mainly Protestants, but a few Catholics – weighed in to advocate:

- segregation of the feeble minded into colonies where their celibacy could be assured;

- compulsory sterilisation;

- restrictions on the immigration of inferior peoples.

The Social Gospel movement (comprising mainly Congregationalist and Unitarian ministers) was particularly active. Their approach was summed up by Rev. Washington Gladden in 1926 as that Christianity 'must be less concerned with getting men to heaven, and more about fitting them for their proper work on Earth.' They saw the controlling of procreation as a valid part of their progressive social reform agenda, and saw eugenics as God's plan to reconcile the truths of science with the bible. They quoted, for example, such passages as the story of Noah's ark, the warning that the sins of the fathers would be visited on descendants, and the

81

parable of the talents, as having clear eugenic messages. This support was enhanced by eugenic sermon contests (with financial prizes) sponsored by the American Eugenics Society.

Between 1908 and 1960, over 60,000 people were compulsorily sterilised in the USA.

Others

Various policies operating within the Commonwealth are worthy of note at this point, notably apartheid and the caste system.

Apartheid (Afrikaans for apartness) was practised by the South African government between 1948 and 1993, and amounted to racial segregation. Hendrick Verwoerd oversaw its introduction and application and it was his government that imprisoned Nelson Mandela (1918 – 2013). In 1962 the United Nations condemned the practice and in 1973/4 it resolved that it was a crime against humanity, and suspended South Africa from membership. In the interim, Verwoerd was murdered in Cape Town in 1966, by an immigrant of mixed race descent.

Interestingly, Mahatma Gandhi was a segregationist and, when he lived in South Africa, he demanded to be allowed to travel first class (normally restricted to whites) and campaigned against having to use the same doors etc. as 'raw Kafffirs'. He counted it a victory when a third door was added to the Durban post office for 'Asiatics' as distinct from Whites or Blacks.

In the 1930's the Belgian government used phrenology to demonstrate the superiority of Tutsis over Hutus – setting the scene for the Rwandan genocide of 1994.

However, none of the above had anything like the impact of Fascism, which we explore in the next chapter.

7. The Fascist era

Influences

We now turn to the developments which undoubtedly explain why the word 'eugenics' has fallen into disrepute, and why Sir Francis Galton is not revered to the extent one would expect based on his achievements. He (like Malthus) had preached a mild form of eugenics: encouraging the eminent to multiply, and discouraging the feeble from doing so, looking for improvements over several generations.

In the aftermath of the First World War (which had brought forward the death of millions of strong and healthy individuals) there were considerable economic problems. The United Kingdom, for example, suffered the General Strike, and was forced to abandon the gold standard, while Germany experienced hyperinflation in which savings were rendered worthless. These and similar experiences saw the topic of eugenics taken in an urgent and aggressive direction, more reminiscent of Plato than Galton, culminating in the emergence of Fascism. As usual, it is helpful to recognise some important influences, as follows.

Arthur de Gobineau 1816 – 1882 was a French aristocrat, famous for developing, in his *Essay on the inequality of the human races*, the theory of Aryan supremacy. He argued that the various races were distinct species. He was opposed to the idea of multi-race imperialism, for fear of degeneration arising from miscegenation.

Friedrich Nietzsche 1844 – 1900 promoted a philosophy that had no need of the 'other worldliness' of religion, but concentrated on 'this worldliness'. Specifically, in *Thus spake Zarathrustra* in 1883, he introduced the idea that, just as the ape had led to man, so man would lead to superman: fearless, masterful and cruel, and

84

filled with 'noble contempt' for the weak, whom he exulted in exterminating. What he called a 'life force' was rooted in the idea that the aspiration of a woman should be to give birth to superior children, and that she should choose her mate accordingly. As we saw in the previous chapter, this was to inspire George Bernard Shaw to write *Man and Superman*. He was of the view that progress required a struggle, and is credited with originating the expression 'What doesn't kill you makes you stronger'.

Vilfredo Pareto (1848 - 1923) attracted attention when, in 1906, he published the results of a survey he had carried out in Italy. It showed that 80% of the land in that country was owned by 20% of the population.

For the mathematically minded, when the frequency of an event is a function of a power of some attribute of that event, it is said to follow a power distribution, and is characteristic of phenomena across a wide field of activity, including geophysical, social and economic. For such distributions, there has to be a number, say k, such that k% of the results come from (100 − k) % of the participants.

What Pareto and others discovered was that the 80:20 power distribution, in particular, applied to so many situations as to warrant being referred to as 'the 80:20 rule'. Specifically, it prompted Pareto to comment that a gulf between the rich and the poor had always been part of the human condition, and that it was a social law in the nature of man that the smarter, abler, stronger and shrewder take the lion's share. On that basis, he argued, democracy was a fraud, in that a ruling class would always emerge and enrich themselves. In other words (those of Giusseppe Prezzolini in 1908), 'History has demonstrated that … there have always been two classes of persons … one dominating, the other dominated'. Such ideas were especially welcome in Pareto's and Prezzolini's homeland, Italy.

[In passing, it is worth noting that, much later, the quality management pioneer Joseph Juran (1904 – 2008) was to pick up Pareto's findings, popularise the idea as 'the vital few and the trivial many' and apply it to a variety of situations, such as 80% of defects being caused by 20% of errors, and 80% of sales being to 20% of customers or of 20% of products. The ratio is still with us today, as with 80% of healthcare costs relating to 20% of population, and 80% of inherited assets going to 20% of inheritors.]

Italy

The first Fascist groups appeared in Italy around 1914, but it was not until 1919 that Benito Mussolini (1883 – 1945) brought them together as a political party. The name was a reference to the Roman fasces – an 'unbreakable' bundle of rods signifying solidarity and state authority. Mussolini began to argue the case for a 'dictatorship based on will and intelligence' and, only three and a half years later, he was invited by King Victor Emmanuel III to become Prime Minister. By 1926, he was established as a one-man dictatorship.

As well as being a prolific writer and orator, Mussolini spoke several languages fluently and was well read (including Machiavelli's *The Prince*, on which he wrote a dissertation). He was by no means regarded as an outsider: at various times, he was subsidised by the French and British governments, who saw him as a bulwark against the spread of communism. He had a close relationship with Austen Chamberlain, the British Foreign Secretary, and it is perhaps worth noting that both Marshal Petain and Neville Chamberlain were members of their respective national Eugenics Societies.

Mussolini was very popular with the Italian population at large, receiving an average of 1,500 letters a day in the 1930's. He was seen as the only man who could control the violence which characterised Italy at that time and, moreover, he was referred to:

- by Adolf Hitler as 'one of the great men on this Earth';

- by Winston Churchill and his wife Clementine as 'one of the most wonderful men of our time';

- by the Daily Mail as 'the saviour of Italy';

- and by no less a person than Pope Pius XI (with whom he signed the Lateran Treaty in 1929, giving the Vatican sovereign status) as 'a man sent by God'.

An interesting aside is that Mussolini tried – but failed - to persuade Pius to excommunicate Hitler from the Catholic Church.

Mussolini defined Fascism (in the *Encyclopedia Italiana*) as 'a religious conception in which man is seen in his immanent relationship with a superior law and with an objective will that transcends the particular individual and raises him to conscious membership of a spiritual society'. Faith and obedience ruled out rationality and criticism.

Fascism rejected both capitalism and communism, positioning itself as a 'third way' (a term revived by Bill Clinton and Tony Blair in the 1990's). In Italy, its approach was that of a 'corporate state' in which workers and employers in a particular major sector were brought together to regulate and modernise their industry. The aim was to organise people in such a way as to produce effective collaboration and to balance the various interests. This was something, as we saw, that Francis Galton had suggested was desirable, and was also endorsed by Pope Pius X1 in *Quadragesimo Anno* published in 1931, when he argued for a reconstruction of economic and political life on the basis of co-operation and solidarity.

However, Fascism was a top-down authoritative concept with strong military style discipline, backed up by violent punishment for miscreants and opponents. It was openly totalitarian (a term coined by the Fascists) in accordance with which trade unions, professions, the police, and even parliament were subordinated to the party. Mussolini, the self-styled *Il Duce*, described democracy as a hindrance to efficient administration. In the difficult conditions after the First World War, Fascism gained considerable popularity as a consequence of its successful intervention in the economy: relieving unemployment by way of public works projects – land reclamation, motorways, hydroelectric power stations and the electrification of the railways - a strategy which chimed with that advocated by Lord Keynes.

In short, his views were reminiscent of the ideas of the Fabians, notably that of an elite dominating the masses. An indication of how 'the centre' of politics has moved is given by the fact that such an approach is now described as 'right wing' – because that is how it appears to people on the (now further) left. It's all relative.

A key presumption underlying Mussolini's policies was his perception that Italy was overpopulated, and therefore needed to conquer, and expand into, neighbouring areas populated by inferior peoples – notably Slav and Mediterranean countries – thereby adhering to the 'natural law' that stronger peoples subject and dominate weaker ones. The Italian race, he asserted, was greater than the Italian state – and nowhere had a history to compare with theirs.   Contrast this with Prince Metternich's dismissal of the peninsular, in 1849, as no more than 'a geographical expression'.

As early as 1928 Mussolini had warned of the danger of the white race being submerged by coloured races which were multiplying much faster and, in 1935/6, he challenged world opinion (as expressed in the League of Nations) by successfully invading Abyssinia, a country he described as barbaric.   This colonisation, characterised by white supremacy and the criminalisation of sexual relations between the races, marked a major shift in his priorities, and was a factor in the build-up to the Second World War.

The number of Jews in Italy was measured in tens of thousands, so anti-Semitism did not feature in his policies; until 1938, that is, when he announced the *Manifesto of Race* - which deprived all members of the Jewish race of their citizenship (and access to various professions etc.) and expelled those who had entered Italy after 1919.   Pius XI had supported the invasion of Abyssinia (and, concurrently, was supporting Franco's 'Falange' Nationalists in Spain) but publicly condemned anti-Semitism as demeaning and divisive.   He was, however, to die in the February of the following year, i.e. a few months before the outbreak of the Second World War.

Mussolini was removed from office in 1943 by the elite (the King, the Fascist Grand Council and large employers) and, after a spell running a government effectively a 'puppet' of Germany, was captured and assassinated in 1945.

The result of the war was a demonstration of the fallacy of 'might is right' basis of Fascism.   Immediately thereafter, history was re-written so as to say that the Italian people had been the victims of a war-mongering leader with minimal public support, and this was enshrined in a 1952 law that made it a criminal offence to 'publically celebrate the exponents, principles, actions or methods of Fascism'. However, as diaries and other writings surfaced in later years, it became clear that the charismatic Mussolini had widespread support (adoration even) thanks to the belief that Fascism had saved the country from ruin, after the degeneration of the early twenties. Fascist laws remained in place until the 1960's.

On the occasion of Holocaust Memorial Day in January 2013, three times Italian Prime Minister Silvio Berlusconi risked prosecution under the 1952 law, having said that, though his anti-Semitism was a mistake forced on him by Hitler, Mussolini 'did good things in so many other areas.'

Indeed, such was the reputation of Fascism in the 1930s that it spawned similar movements in Argentina, Brazil, Hungary, Portugal, Romania and others. In Spain, it led to a brutal civil war, but the most earth-shattering was the rise of Nazism in Germany.

Germany

Developments in Germany between the wars were influenced by all the writers mentioned earlier – including Sir Francis Galton, it has to be said - but two others are worthy of note.

Houston Stewart Chamberlain 1855 – 1927 was British by birth but German by naturalisation (in 1916) and married Eva, daughter of Richard Wagner (whose words and music were popular with the Nazi elite). In 1899, he published *The Foundations of the nineteenth century* (described by George Bernard Shaw as a 'historical masterpiece'). It was to become a strong influence on the pan-Germanic movement (embracing imperialism, anti-Semitism and a belief that Germans were a superior race which justified the conquering of inferior ones). In it, he positioned Germans at the helm of the Aryan race – and

90

indeed all races, and – echoing Galton - asserted that the decline of such outstanding civilisations as ancient Greece and Rome had been a consequence of inter-racial marriages. In other publications he denounced the concept of parliamentary government.

Alfred Rosenberg, 1893-1946 was a Baltic German, born in Estonia. He provided a philosophical and religious basis for the German National Socialist party of which he was, from its formation, an active and senior member. He himself had been influenced by the ideas of Houston Stewart Chamberlain, and advanced them in the form of a racial 'ladder'. This had blacks and Jews at the bottom and Aryans (a label subject to a variable definition) at the top. He condemned what he called 'negative Christianity' (on account of its Jewish roots) and argued for a 'positive Christianity', in which Jesus was an Aryan who had lived in an enclave in Galilee and struggled against Judaism. In 1930, he published *The myth of the twentieth century,* a book on racial theory. He advocated an increase in the birth rate of racially pure Aryans, persecution of the Jews, opposition to liberal imperialism and Marxism, and abrogation of the Versailles Treaty. At the conclusion of the war, he was tried as a war criminal, found guilty, and hanged.

1923 is a key date, in that a Nazi attempt to seize control in Germany, known as the Munich Beer Hall Putsch, failed, and the leader of the party, **Adolf Hitler (1889 – 1945)**, was found guilty of treason. He was sentenced to five years' imprisonment - but served only nine months, during which he wrote *Mein Kampf.* Much of the philosophy therein was based on the ideas covered earlier.

Specifically, he saw human life as a competitive struggle for existence, in which Providence gives the Earth to the best people. Nature, he argued, does not concentrate her attentions on preserving what exists, but on breeding offspring to carry on the species. In return, those best people were obligated to promote the victory of the better and stronger and the subordination of the weaker. He saw the pan-German race (a concept greater than that of the German state at that time, and roughly correlated with use of the German language) as clearly superior to all others.

The importance of this rested on his view that, like Italy, Germany faced a problem of overpopulation, which would bring catastrophe if not dealt with. He rejected some of the proffered solutions, such as:

- generalised birth control, as it circumvented the struggle for existence needed to strengthen a race; and

- peaceful economic conquest based on superior efficiency and trade surpluses [as practiced by Germany since the war to the present day] as being subject to tight limits.

Rather, on the grounds that the German race was the highest form of humanity, he advocated a two-fold solution: the acquisition of additional territory in Europe, and the weeding out of undesirables.

Only the healthy should beget children, and this should not be limited by financial pressures. The most beautiful bodies should be able to find each other. The state must act as guardian of a millennial future for the race, in which the wishes of the individual should appear as nothing. As part of that process, some people must be declared unfit for propagation. Defectives must be prevented from propagating defective offspring. The pitifully sick had to be segregated – this was unfortunate for them, but a blessing for others and for posterity. The goal was the preservation and improvement of the race.

The same 'basic aristocratic principle of Nature' meant that the leadership should fall to the best minds, to whom the broad masses should be subordinated. Absolute responsibility should be matched by unconditional authority: decisions are made by individuals, albeit after seeking advice from people with specialist knowledge. He was, therefore, anti-parliamentarian, being especially critical of the principle of majority rule as encouraging compromise and discouraging independent thought. Even the Nazis' participation in parliamentary institutions was (openly) only for the purpose of their destruction.

Consequently, he was unashamedly totalitarian, with a vision of the Party embracing the state, and covering all the main issues of the day. Institutions such as the professions and trade unions had to be placed in the service of a moral, political and cultural idea. Likewise with education: the young must learn to obey, and thereby acquire a basis for commanding. [Here I have to confess that the official song of my grammar school (Queen Mary's, Walsall) contains the symbolic line 'Only by obedience may we learn to rule'.]

All this called for a top-down, command and compliance approach to organisation, the leader of each subgroup being appointed from above. His mantra was 'transforming philosophy into action' and his watchwords 'Ein volk, ein reich, ein fuhrer' (one people, one state, one leader). Talent needed to be identified in each generation, and used in the service of the community. For that reason, he departed from Galton's thinking, to praise the Catholic Church for its celibacy policy which forced it to search for talent in each generation, and its use of dogma to prevent wasting time on pointless argument.

A key feature of his philosophy was that the concepts of states / nations should not be described in terms of economics. Rather, he defined a community as being an organisation of physically and psychologically similar living beings with the aim of preserving and improving the race. In this, the individual must sacrifice himself for the totality – a philosophy which was encapsulated in the claim that his was the thousand year Reich. The state represents not an end, but a means to the end of improving the race. He explained the success of Christianity in terms of its fanaticism in fighting for its doctrine. He admired the Ancient Greeks and accepted Francis Galton's explanation that their decline was attributable to racial mixing with inferior people.

Hitler became Chancellor in 1933, and what have been described as eugenic laws then came thick and fast. In April of that year, the government declared a boycotting of Jewish businesses. Then 1934 saw the introduction of the Sterilisation Law, allowing for the sterilisation of undesirables, notably those with hereditary illnesses, but also habitual offenders against public morals (including racial pollution). Hitler told his comrades just how closely he had followed the progress of the American eugenics movement. He said that he had studied with great interest the laws of several American states concerning the 'prevention of reproduction by people whose progeny would, in all probability, be of no value or be injurious to the racial stock.'

The feeling was mutual, especially in California, where the mood was summed up by the eugenics leader C. M. Goeth who, on returning from Germany in 1934, noted that more than 5,000 people per month were being forcibly sterilized. 'You will be interested to know' he wrote to a colleague, 'that your work has played a powerful part in shaping the opinions of the group of intellectuals who are behind Hitler in this epoch-making program. Everywhere I sensed that their opinions have been tremendously stimulated by American thought . . . I want you, my dear friend, to carry this thought with you for the rest of your life, that you have really jolted into action a great government of 60 million people.'

At the same time, a U.K. Department of Health report, from a committee chaired by Sir Lawrence Brock, praised the Nazi legislation and urged the adoption of something similar here. As late as 1938, the U.S. news magazine *Time* was to select Adolph Hitler as their 'Man of the year' in recognition of the unification of Germany with Austria and the Sudetenland (and followed this up by selecting Joseph Stalin for the same honour in 1939).

Meanwhile, in 1935, came the Nuremberg Laws, which divided Germans into two categories: citizens with full rights, and subjects with few rights – and outlawed sexual intercourse between the categories. These laws led to the persecution of various 'international' groupings, including Jews (people were required to produce family trees to prove that they were not even a quarter Jewish), Gypsies, Jehovah's Witnesses, and Freemasons, all of which were seen as competitors for people's loyalties.

Hitler frequently highlighted the yoke of international capitalism – and its masters, the Jews. A symptom of decay had been the slow disappearance of private property, and the growth of joint stock corporations. He believed that the Jews were racially inferior, playing a decisive role in various social ills. In the Reichstag in January 1939, he promised that 'If the international Jewish financiers should succeed in plunging nations once more into a world war, then the result will not be the Bolshevisation of the earth but the annihilation of the Jewish race in Europe.'

Also around this time, interest in euthanasia began to expand rapidly. The main argument related to the costs of caring for unproductive lives – the mentally ill, the old and infirm, etc. Hitler approved of euthanasia in principle, as a means of relieving incompetent people of 'the burden of life'. Hundreds of thousands of so called 'mercy killings' occurred over the next few years. In 1941, the idea was extended to those in concentration camps who were incapable of work – or simply enemies of the Party – and then to wounded soldiers. Extermination camps, located in Poland, supervised the deaths of millions. Key figures in this programme were as follows.

Otmar Freiherr von Verschuer 1896 – 1969 who was a director of the Kaiser Wilhelm Institute for Anthropology, Human Heredity and Eugenics in Berlin, established by someone we have met earlier: Eugen Fischer (what an apt forename for the man who had experimented on the Herero tribe in Namibia) and, later, at the Institute for Hereditary Biology and Racial Hygiene at Frankfurt. His work on twins was funded by donations from the Rockefeller Foundation. With permission from SS Reichsführer Heinrich Himmler, he began 'anthropological testing' of inmates at Auschwitz concentration camp (designated by the Nazis as the place of the final solution of the Jewish question in Europe). Around 1.5 million people died there, 90% of them Jewish, by way of gas chambers, starvation, execution, and medical experiments. Verscheur was never tried for war crimes, and in 1951 he was appointed as a professor of human genetics at the University of Munster. He was a member of the American Eugenics Society until his death (in a road accident).

Joseph Mengele 1911-1979 had worked for Eugen Fischer and, for a long time, as assistant to Verschuer. At Auschwitz, he was known as the Angel of Death, for his role as the camp physician tasked with deciding which arrivals would be treated as forced labourers and which sent to the gas chamber. He would also seek out twins and pregnant women, on whom he would carry out surgical experiments (often causing their death) in pursuit of his interest in heredity. After the war, he escaped to South America, where he lived for over thirty years.

Heinrich Himmler 1900 – 1945 oversaw the implementation of the holocaust, leading to the deaths of around 6 million Jews, and almost as many others, such as Gypsies and Slavs. He committed suicide in 1945.

After the war, the Nazi version of eugenics was declared a crime against humanity - an act of genocide. Germans were tried and they cited the California statutes, and the judgement in Buck v Bell in their defence, but to no avail: they were found guilty.

But the record of National Socialism lives on. 80 years, to the day, after Hitler came to power, Chancellor Angela Merkel warned that social divisions could allow such tyranny to return. The rise of the Nazis, she said, 'was made possible because the elite of German society worked with them but also, above all, because most in Germany tolerated this rise'.

Great Britain and Ireland

Sir Oswald Mosley (1896 – 1980) was a member of an Anglo-Irish family, seated at Rolleston Hall, near Burton on Trent, and was a fourth cousin of Queen Elizabeth the Queen Mother (wife of King George VI and mother of Queen Elizabeth II). His first marriage, in 1920, was to Lady Cynthia Curzon (daughter of Lord Curzon, Viceroy of India, and later Foreign Secretary); both were committed Fabians. His second marriage, in 1936, was to Diana Mitford, whose grandfather, Lord Redesdale, had written the preface to the English version of Houston Chamberlain's book on the nineteenth century. The wedding was attended by Adolf Hitler, a close friend of both Diana and her sister Unity Valkyrie Mitford (who shot herself – though not fatally - when war broke out). Moseley became Conservative member for Harrow in 1918 and held it as an independent before joining the Independent Labour

Party in 1924. In 1926, he won a by-election in Smethwick, and went on to join the cabinet.

Following a policy disagreement in 1931, he formed the New Party, and visited Italy to study Fascism – deciding that it was the way forward for Britain, which prompted him to form the British Union of Fascists in 1932. The party was regularly involved in violent confrontations with Jews and Communists, and instituted a corps of black shirted stewards. For most of the Second World War, he was interned, as were his wife and other active fascists. He attempted to return to politics after the war, majoring on the problems brought about by immigration, but with little success: he was a parliamentary candidate in a couple of constituencies in London, but lost his deposits.

Thus it was that 'eugenics' came to mean something distasteful. However, the original concept, the underlying ideas, and the identified problems did not go away with the ending of the Second World War – as we shall now see. Various developments from 1945 to the present day chime with the concept of eugenics. They are very interdependent but, for ease of assimilation, I have grouped them under four headings: politics, medical, education and population.

8. The politics of elites and masses

A drift to the left

Though the two main parties – Conservative and Labour – have moved in and out of office since the end of the Second World War, the direction of travel has been mainly towards the left of the political spectrum. The late Peter Mair wrote about the 'cartelisation' of politics, in the sense that the parties 'pursue a form of competition that is so lacking in meaning, that they no longer seem capable of sustaining democracy in its present form.'

The extent of the shift can be quantified in that, prior to the First World War, government expenditure in the United Kingdom amounted to less than 10% of National Income; since the Second World War, it has hovered around the 50% mark.

The most significant shift had its roots in the need to mobilise for two world wars, and to cope with economic crises between them, prompting central government to take on a much larger role in the affairs of the nation - and this was not unwound on the cessation of hostilities. Indeed, somewhat ironically, immediately after having fought a debilitating war against National Socialism, the U.K. population elected the Labour party whose platform was unequivocally … national socialism.

Over 200 members of the Fabian Society were elected to parliament in 1945, many to hold high office, including Prime Minister, Clement - later Earl - Attlee (1883 - 1967) who had worked for a time as secretary to Beatrice Webb, and lectured at the London School of Economics. Chairman of the party at that time was Harold Laski (1893 – 1950) who in 1910 had published a paper entitled *The scope of eugenics*, which had brought praise from Sir Francis Galton himself.

Attlee had outlined his political principles in his 1920 book *The Social Worker*. In a key section, he dismissed two ways of dealing with the disadvantaged - neglect (inhumane) and charity (demeaning) - in favour of state care funded by taxation. 'Charity is a cold grey loveless thing. If a rich man wants to help the poor, he should pay his taxes gladly, not dole out money at a whim'. He genuinely hoped that charitable institutions would 'wither on the vine' but the fact is they haven't.

He was opposed to *international* socialism in general: he would shudder at today's phenomenon of 'benefit tourism' where foreigners are attracted by Britain's welfare system, and the billions of pounds allocated to overseas aid. Specifically, he was opposed to the Soviet Union, and his government began the process of dismantling the Empire by granting independence to its largest constituent: the Indian subcontinent.

At home, the government embarked on a massive restructuring, under three main headings, as follows.

- **Nationalisation**. By the late nineteen forties, 'public ownership' had been extended to coal mines, railways, road haulage and canals, iron and steel, electricity, gas, civil aviation, telecommunications and the Bank of England. Trade Unions were supportive of nationalisation, on the grounds that it provided greater job security and higher wages. The other side of the coin showed reduced responsiveness to change which, coupled with a lack of investment, led to inefficiencies.

- **The welfare state**. The mantra was that the state would take care of the population 'from the cradle to the grave', comprising the National Health Service ('free at the point of delivery'), unemployment and sickness benefits (marking the end of workhouses), family allowances, home help, retirement benefits and even funeral benefits. Meanwhile, the government

100

mounted a massive, subsidised investment in social housing: 80% of the 1 million houses built between 1945 and 1951 were council houses.

- **Taxation**. The Labour government was committed to substantial redistribution of wealth, which was pursued by way of a 'Robin Hood' approach, i.e. weakening the strong in order to support the weak, typified by very progressive income tax (with a top rate of 90%) and death duties (80%).

This was the biggest move towards a collectivist state in the history of the United Kingdom, and took the country a long way from the idea of a market economy which had been a defining feature of the growth of the nation, and rationing continued throughout the Labour Party's tenure of office.

A remarkably prescient education booklet entitled *The struggle for democracy*, published by Cadbury Brothers Limited in 1944 (at which time the Cadburys were substantial financial supporters of Liberalism) highlighted the potential problems inherent in socialism, summed up in the following questions.

- 'When we pay out of our pockets, we count the cost. Do we think so carefully before helping ourselves to the benefits provided by the state?'

- 'With full employment, fewer people fear poverty, or are afraid of losing their jobs. Will there now be less incentive to work hard?'

- 'People who work hardest and earn the most are penalised by taxation. Can the government devise taxation which is not a fine for hard work?'

- 'Without competition, which in the past has contributed to low prices and good service, what will the result be?'

- 'There is a gap between what our exports earn and what our imports cost. We must reduce our dependence on America [in the form of Marshall Aid].' The reality was that the pound was devalued by 30% in 1949 (from $4 to $2.80).

Those questions are no less valid or urgent today than they were then.

Financial pressures

As we saw in chapter 6, one of the foundations of the welfare state was the Beveridge report which, in turn, centred on the introduction of a comprehensive, compulsory insurance scheme, based on a universal flat rate contribution, which would determine the extent to which benefits could be claimed. Specifically, on unemployment, he said that benefits should not be so high as to deter people from getting a job. This was the way, he argued, that would ensure that work would pay, saving would be encouraged, and a dependency culture would be avoided.

However, health and welfare were never put onto a funded basis; from the start, current contributions went towards defraying current expenditure, the deficit being covered by government borrowing. As the years went by, this situation was exacerbated, not least as a consequence of the massive strides made in pharmaceuticals and surgical procedures. Longevity has increased, meaning that an ever increasing proportion of the population is entitled to state pensions. As a percentage of Gross National Product, government spending on health and welfare has more than doubled.

Successive governments have responded to the situation in various ways, notably by reducing the scope of the schemes (e.g. drastically reducing optometry and dentistry, and charging for prescriptions) and abandoning the idea of a flat rate contribution, in favour of a (steadily increasing) percentage of income. At the same time, they have moved away from the idea that benefits should be determined by contributions, substituting the communist concept of 'from each according to his ability, to each according to his need'. One does not need an economics degree to see that taxing employment and subsidising unemployment can have only an adverse effect on aggregate employment and output.

This is far removed from the principles enunciated by Beveridge, and has had the predictable result of hundreds of thousands of people choosing to live off their fellow citizens via the benefit system – and seeing it as an entitlement, sometimes embracing three generations in a household. In interviews it is explained that it is largely about the margin – the *extra* income from working is so small as to be seen as not worth the effort. At the same time, housing and child benefits are so attractive that young women brought up in a workless environment see life as a single parent (often of several children) as a career choice. A quarter of people under the age of 18 in the U.K. are being reared by a single parent – the second highest ratio in Europe after Latvia.

Bizarrely, the historical aversion to 'means testing' has meant that many millions of people pay taxes *and* receive benefits. Winter heating allowances, free television licences and travel passes for the elderly, and the hideously complex working tax credits are good examples. How inefficient to give people back (some of) their own money - the defence that it creates employment for civil servants is unacceptable.

103

As early as 1997, the then Prime Minister, Tony Blair, asserted that 'We have reached the limits of the public's willingness to fund an unreformed welfare system through ever higher taxes and spending'. He invited Frank Field to 'think the unthinkable' but what he thought was politically unacceptable, and the problem continued to get worse, exacerbated by high unemployment which has added to the costs while reducing tax receipts.

By the time the Conservative / Liberal Coalition came into being in 2010, there was considerable support for a move back to a funded contributory scheme. In tune with that mood, Iain Duncan Smith, Secretary of State for Work and Pensions, talked about the benefit system 'promoting destructive behaviour' by encouraging poorer families to have more children than the wealthy, and denying them an incentive to work. He reminded people that Beveridge had said that those on benefits cannot hope to receive assistance from a bottomless pit, a principle which is especially so when economy is shrinking and public finances are under pressure.

All this has led not only to high costs (health and welfare account for over £350 billion per annum), but created a divided society: the prudent are irritated when they see the feckless getting free care. A Galtonian view was encapsulated in a letter to the *Daily Telegraph* in April 2011, from a lady who argued that the government ought to encourage higher rate tax payers to produce more higher-rate tax payers. 'When I want to have another baby, I do so at my cost' she wrote, but 'when someone on benefits wants to have another baby, she gets paid to do so, again at my cost.'

Elitism again

In his 2010 book, *The servile mind: how democracy erodes the moral life*, Professor Kenneth Minogue (1930 – 2013) addressed 'the remarkable fact that, while democracy means a government accountable to the electorate, our rulers make us more accountable to them'. He went on to argue that politicians 'have no business telling us how to live' and that 'we should be in no doubt that nationalising the moral life is the first step towards totalitarianism.'

Early on in the life of the coalition elected in 2010, various symptoms of totalitarianism became exposed by the ramifications of the 'hacking scandal', notably the discovery of collusion involving politicians, the press and the police. Adding to this situation, a review commissioned by the BBC Trust reported in July 2013 that the Corporation had been so closely attuned to the views of the government that they had been slow to reflect the weight of public concern regarding such issues as:

- the U.K.'s membership of the European Community;

- the scale of immigration;

- the appeal of the U.K. Independence Party.

Edmund Burke, elected as a Whig for Bristol in 1774 famously argued that 'Your representative owes you not his industry, but his judgement – the mature judgement of natural aristocracy.' What Galton was to favourably acknowledge as the *vox populi*, Burke saw as 'the tyranny of the multitude'. Many voters think the 'Chartist' view is preferable, i.e. that MPs should be representatives (not delegates) of the people and should reflect their views, and this may be more feasible now, given the vast amount of information online, coupled with the way social media have developed.

The minimum wage

As we saw in chapter 6, the early Fabians were staunch eugenicists, and one of their innovations was the idea of the minimum wage, as a means of excluding the 'unfit' from the labour force, by pricing then out of the labour market (because the value of their output is inadequate, or machines can do the job more cheaply).

Somewhere along the line, however, the idea was appropriated by politicians who thought it would be a good way of increasing the standard of living of workers, reducing poverty and inequality, in such a way that the bill was picked up by businesses rather than the state. It was formally introduced in 1999, and the actual rate is reviewed every autumn. Meanwhile, anti-poverty campaigners are urging the government to embrace the concept of a 'living wage' significantly above the minimum wage.

However, the application of even the minimum wage has an adverse effect on employment, As its proponents could have been told by any first year economics student, increasing the price of anything has an adverse effect on demand. Confusion reigned within the Coalition government, as evidenced by contrary advice:

- In April 2013, the Department for Business changed the terms of reference of the Low Pay Commission so as to specify a goal of raising the wages of the lowest paid *without damaging employment or the economy.*

- In January 2014, the Chancellor asked the Low Pay Commission to consider the case for a significant increase in the minimum wage – ostensibly to help the less well-off through the economic crisis, and reinforce the message that work pays, but seen as raw party politics.

Troubled families

Following the riots in the summer of 2011, the Prime Minister set up the 'Troubled Families Unit'. The focus was on around

120,000 families that cost the taxpayer around £9 billion a year in benefits, crime, antisocial behaviour, child care and healthcare. The aim was to turn their lives around by 2015, involving getting children back into school, reducing youth crime and antisocial behaviour, and getting adults back into work. This was to be done by joining up local services, and appointing a single key worker who would deal with a family's problems as a whole, not individually.

By the summer of 2012, the head of the unit, Louise Casey, was expressing the view that mothers of large problem families (a fifth of the 120,000 have more than five children) should be ashamed of the damage they are doing to society, and stop having children when they are struggling to cope with the ones they have. Mothers with large families should take responsibility and stop getting pregnant (often, she noted, by different men).

In May 2013 The Centre for Social Justice published a report which noted that around seven million people lived in 'welfare ghettos' where more than half of those of working age are on benefit. That figure included two million children, most of whom had no concept of a job. The most popular ambitions were to be boss of a gang or a celebrity. One in five children in the UK is growing up in a workless household – the second highest ratio in Europe after Macedonia.

A particularly contentious topic is care in old age, given that the population as a whole (including the government) is putting insufficient away for its dotage. In February 2013, prompted by the findings of the Dilnot enquiry, the government announced that the costs of care in old age were to be capped at £75,000 'in order to 'end the scandal' of people having to cash in their savings and / or sell their house in order to pay for care. But some would query whether this is a scandal. The effect of the new policy is to allow more assets to be passed on to children – and the inheritance tax threshold is being reduced in real terms in order to help fund the new policy.

The European dimension

In an agreement which paved the way for the Treaty of Rome (1957) the six members of the European Steel and Coal Community declared their aim as being to 'further progress towards the setting up of a united Europe through the development of common institutions, the gradual merging of national economies, the creation of a common market and the harmonisation of social policies'. This was achieved through the Single European Act (1986) the Maastricht Treaty (1992) and the Lisbon Treaty (2007).

In a statement reminiscent of George Bernard Shaw's strategy as quoted in chapter 6, however, the Right Honourable Peter Thorneycroft advised his colleagues in the Conservative Party that 'no government dependent on a democratic vote could possibly agree in advance to the sacrifices which any plan for European Union must involve. The people must be led, slowly and unconsciously …. not asked.' This was obviously taken on board by Prime Minister Ted Heath (who signed the treaty taking the country into the European Economic Community in 1972) when, in a television interview, he said that 'there are some in this country who fear that, by going into Europe, we shall in some way sacrifice independence and sovereignty. Those fears, I need hardly say, are completely unjustified.'

The early Fabians would have been delighted with the way the European Union project was 'never called by its proper name' but sold as simply a common market. Even in 1975, when Harold

Wilson called a referendum, the question was specifically whether or not people wanted to 'stay in the Common Market'.

Speaking to the Trade Unions Congress in 1988, the then president of the European Commission Jacques Delors reassured them that, if overt socialism was a political liability in the U.K., there was an alternative. By going over the heads of voters, to Brussels, they could ally themselves with fellow travellers, who were not accountable to the electorate. Whereas previously there had been no support within the Labour party for the European project, suddenly it became – and has remained - a key feature of its policy.

There has never been any consultation on what was clearly its founders' determination, namely to elevate it to a Community and then Union, empowering unelected bureaucrats to prescribe laws and practices with which member states must conform. To quote the late Peter Mair again, political elites have been rendered 'safe from the demands of voters and their representatives.'

Conversely, the President of the European Commission, Jose Manuel Barroso, speaking in 2010 argued that 'If governments were always right, we wouldn't have the situation we have today. Decisions taken by the most democratic institutions in the world are often wrong'. Pareto would agree with him, but it would be risky to assume that unaccountable bureaucrats always get things right.

Within the Union, a group of countries have been defying the lessons of history and struggling to maintain a currency union based on the euro. This has caused enormous problems for countries on the southern periphery, notably Greece, Italy, Spain and Portugal. The overriding question is whether it is right that the burden of adjustment should be borne by those heavily indebted countries themselves.

One of the consequences of that policy has been the emergence, in those struggling countries, of fascist political groups. Golden Dawn, for example, openly racialist and anti-democratic, took third place in the Greek elections in 2012, with 7% of the vote, only to be proscribed as a criminal organisation.

Remembering Lord Keynes' comments on the First World War reparations, and on the Bretton Woods agreement, we can safely say that he would advocate a very different solution, i.e. that the debtors should be bailed out by the prosperous north (notably Germany, which has followed the 'superior productivity leading to massive surpluses' strategy described but rejected by Hitler). Either way, the European Union founders' claims that it would enhance wealth across the board, and improve inter-country relations seem a long way from the current reality.

European Commission research, published in 2014, acknowledged that there were over 600,000 'non-active migrants' in the United Kingdom but insisted that it is unlawful to discriminate against them (relative to the indigenous population) as regards welfare benefits. Other countries are able to discriminate, because their systems are contributory but, since ours are no longer so, the Commission argues, we shouldn't. A solution suggests itself.

One is reminded of Alexis de Tocqueville's explanation of the French revolution: 'the aristocracy fell into contempt because they claimed privileges on the basis of functions they could no longer fulfil'.

9. Medical developments

What's in a name?

We noted earlier that, though Galton's concept of eugenics was patient and long term, the preaching and practices of the Fabians and Fascists were impatient and urgent. Unfortunately, it was the latter which came to dominate thinking, to the point that 'eugenics' was seen a synonymous with the Nazi philosophy of the master race and its consequent atrocities.

This prompted supporters to indulge in a bout of name changing:

- the Eugenics Society became The Galton Institute;

- its American equivalent became The Society for the Study of Social Biology;

- and the expression 'birth control' was replaced by 'family planning'.

Genetics

Genetics is a subset of biology, the noun being coined by William Bateson in 1905. It covers the study of genes, which determine how a living organism inherits traits from its ancestors and owes much to the work of Gregor Mendel, as mentioned in chapter 4, especially his identification of dominant and recessive genes.

Post war developments have been enormous, notably the discovery in 1958, by James Watson and Francis Crick, of the helical structure of DNA (deoxyribonucleic acid) which contain units that line up, in a particular order, information for constructing and operating a living organism; and the Human Genome Project which ran from 1997 to 2003.

This is not the place for a detailed coverage of the enormous strides made in this subject, but we might note ones with a bearing on eugenics as follows.

- The running of tests designed to show up predisposition – on account of heredity - to particular illnesses. However, this has brought ethical concerns, e.g. how such knowledge might be used to discriminate against people as regards employment and insurance. Also, whether the discoverers should be allowed to patent modified genes: would this amount to a reward for investment, or holding health services to ransom?

- Genetic engineering, under which genes can be replaced or inserted to combat inherited weaknesses.

- In conjunction with *in vitro* fertilisation (see below)

- Genetic fingerprinting, which was discovered by Sir Alec Jeffries, a professor at the University of Leicester, in 1984. Its value came to be widely recognised in 1988 when it was used in the conviction of Colin Pitchfork for the murder of two girls in Leicestershire. It was also given publicity in 1992 when skeletons found in a shallow grave in Russia were positively identified by the Forensic Science Service as the last Tsar, his wife, and 3 children. In 2002, its profiling discriminating power was raised to 1 in 1 billion.

- Galton's theory that inheritance was about characteristics being passed from embryo to embryo provided the foundation for further advances in our understanding of heredity, as popularised in Richard Dawkins' *The selfish gene* which positioned the struggle for existence at the level of the gene.

Family planning

This remains a subject of fierce debate between the pro-life camp (who see termination of pregnancy as the destruction of a human life) and pro-choice camp (who see it as the solution to the problem of an unwanted pregnancy).

One of the most far-reaching developments was that of the contraceptive pill, the early funding for which came from the Rockefeller Foundation. More recently, we have seen the arrival of the morning-after pill, available to over 16s. This was originally seen as an emergency, but its usage is currently over 200,000 per annum. The British Pregnancy Advice Service (BPAS) which runs a number of abortion clinics advises women to stock up with morning after pills, with suitability being determined by way of a phone call.

Abortion

For centuries, abortion was positioned as a criminal offence in the United Kingdom but, after the Second World War, opinions began to change, not least thanks to the work of the BPAS.

The Abortion Act of 1967, as subsequently amended and affected by others, legalised abortion up to 24 weeks (or more in the case of 'grave' problems), by a registered medical practitioner, provided that two such practitioners agree in good faith that (a) continuance would increase the risk of injury to the physical or mental health of the pregnant woman or her other children; or (b) there is a substantial risk that the child would suffer such abnormalities as to be seriously handicapped.

The BPAS had been founded in 1968 in Birmingham and, on the day the Act came into force, the first patients had their consultations. The organization has always argued that women are best placed to decide whether or not to continue with a pregnancy.

Over the years, the number of abortions has increased substantially; currently, in the U.K. it is running at 190,000 per annum (compared with around 800,000 births). There is considerable support for the view that abortion is being seen as a back-up, when contraception has failed, so as to manage the size and timing families to suit circumstances. It seems to be the case that the woman's wishes are seldom refused: all she has to do in order to establish mental health grounds is to threaten suicide. Meanwhile, the Church of England view is that 'as soon as there is an individual, there is a person ... but ... there are some situations in which abortion is the lesser evil'.

The matter was brought to a head in early 2012, when it was revealed that a substantial proportion of terminations were initiated on the grounds of the sex of the unborn child. Supporters argue that women have a right to know the sex of their unborn child, and to choose whether or not to continue the pregnancy. Sometimes this is simply a matter of 'family balancing'. However, the issue seems to be socially and politically sensitive because of the ethnic dimension: in some cultures boys are valued more highly than girls, and aborting girls is regarded as acceptable practice.

The exposure of these practices led to the resignation of the chief executive of the Care Quality Commission but, later, that body undertook an enquiry, based on unannounced visits, and reported that there was clear evidence that fourteen hospitals had used forms that had been pre-signed by one doctor, for use by another (circumventing the requirement for two doctors to agree that the risk of carrying on a pregnancy is greater than that of an abortion). The Health Secretary said that anyone found to be breaking the law would be reported to the police and the General Medical Council ('GMC').

After an 18-month investigation, the Crown Prosecution Service concluded that, though there was sufficient evidence to bring charges, and a realistic chance of securing a conviction, they had decided that it would not be in the public interest to do so. Their main reasons for doing so, they said, were that doctors had wide discretion with regard to interpreting the law, and that the GMC was still investigating the matter – appearing to put the profession above the law. When the GMC reported, it was to say that, although it is normally unethical to terminate a pregnancy on the grounds of foetal gender alone, the woman's views on its effect on her situation and on her existing children should nevertheless be considered. The Director of Public Prosecutions interpreted this advice as saying that, if a woman said that she would be seriously affected by giving birth to a girl, that would provide legal and ethical justification for a termination, and ruled, therefore, that abortions on the grounds of gender were not prohibited by law.

In December 2013, it emerged that fewer than half of women who had abortions in 2012 had actually seen either of the doctors who signed their authorisations, and a government consultation paper suggested that this reality should be recognised in official guidance, i.e. it is not a legal requirement for doctors to actually see women requesting an abortion; the process can be overseen by nurses (who are likely to be better able to deal with the emotional and psychological aspects).

That seemed to clarify the matter but then, in May 2014, the Health Secretary announced new guidance that declared that gender-based abortion and the pre-signing of consent forms are 'unacceptable and illegal'. Thus the situation remains murky, and is likely to become more so, as medical science allows more potential problems to be identified in the foetus – but, by the same token, according to ministers, the abortion limit in the UK could be lowered.

In Vitro Fertilisation ('IVF')

We now turn to situations at the other end of the scale, namely ones in which conception does not come naturally. From a purely eugenic point of view, this would prompt the thought that nature might be thereby preventing a genetic problem arising. On the other hand, the evidence is that infertility is a source of anguish and sadness, and has led to marital break-ups and mental illness. For this reason, it is recognised as a medical condition by the World Health Organisation.

Science has produced a response in the form of IVF, which is a procedure whereby an egg is fertilised by sperm outside the body, then returned to the woman's uterus in the expectation of a normal pregnancy. The process was pioneered by Doctors Steptoe and Edwards at Bourn Hall Fertility Clinic, leading to the birth of the world's first 'test tube baby', Louise Brown, in 1978.

Since then, it has become increasingly popular, with an estimated 5 million babies having been born after IVF, worldwide. It seems to have a particular appeal for women choosing to delay child bearing, so as to pursue a career. Currently, around 60,000 cycles of treatment are carried out each year in the UK, and now account for 2% of births nationwide.

Under guidelines issued by The National Institute for Health and Clinical Excellence, the treatment is available on the National Health Service, funded out of general taxation, but there is a 'postcode lottery' as many Trusts impose further hurdles, and some do not fund any IVF at all. Coupled with the fact that success rates on the NHS are relatively low (seen as being due to the fact that

116

NHS staff are too busy to get the timing of the various steps just right) the majority of procedures are still privately funded. This naturally raises the concern that it is 'the preserve of the well-off'.

In practice, the procedure is not restricted to married couples, but can be obtained by single people, and those in same-sex relationships. This is opposed by the Catholic Church on the religious grounds that it separates reproduction from marriage.

Another feature of the science is that eggs can be genetically screened and selected – some being discarded and others having material known to be responsible for some hereditary illnesses or disabilities replaced. Supporters argue that exercising our ability to screen out flaws amounts to good parenting, but opponents say that it is immoral to choose which embryo to fertilise.

The practice of 'surrogacy' has also developed, in which the fertilised egg is implanted in a 'gestational carrier' who will carry the pregnancy to term – but the baby is the biological child of the provider of the egg. Commercial surrogacy is illegal in the United Kingdom, but is allowed in some American states. More recently, an unusual industry has been spawned, within which Indian women earn relatively large sums for what is known as 'outsourced surrogacy'. This involves Eastern European eggs and Western European sperm brought together in an American laboratory, then implanted in the wombs of the Indian women.

In September 2012, the issue was taken to a new level of complexity and controversy, with the publication of a consultation paper, by the Human Fertilisation and Embryology Authority, on the notion that a child could be born containing the DNA from three parents: genes from father and mother, and mitochondrial DNA from an unrelated female egg donor, the aim being to eliminate identified risks of disability. However, the Council of Europe, a human rights organisation, condemned the idea as being 'tantamount to eugenics (!) and incompatible with human dignity and international law.'

Death control

Medical science has reached the point where people are kept alive even though they no longer have any quality of life. In a hospital situation, relatives were for some time able to acquiesce to what was known as the *Liverpool Care Pathway* (having been developed at the Marie Curie hospice on Merseyside) which kept patients comfortable by way of medication (usually increasing doses of morphine) but reduced sustenance. This allowed them to slip away peacefully and with dignity. The Medical Ethics Alliance argued that this amounted to an abandonment of 'evidence based medicine', given that there is no scientific way of diagnosing imminent death. A difficult aspect was that, quite often, the number of patients put on to the pathway was one of the measures of performance which influenced funding. Furthermore, when some members of the public gave examples of its inappropriate use, saying that informed consent was not always being sought, the Government decided to suspend it in the summer of 2013, and to develop a more consultative system.

Beyond that is the question of assisted dying, where people themselves seek help to die. Currently, this is illegal in the United Kingdom. However, the Commission on Assisted Dying (set up and funded by prominent members of 'Dignity in Dying') argued that the law should be changed to allow people with less than twelve months to live, who request it, and who are deemed to have the mental capacity to make that decision, to be prescribed drugs to hasten their end. To safeguard the vulnerable, those with disabilities, dementia or depression would not be allowed to request it, but opponents say it would be the thin end of the wedge.

Speaking to the Church of England Synod in February 2012, the Archbishop of Canterbury warned that moves to legalise assisted suicide could spell disaster for society, causing problems for vulnerable people, and for doctors. He drew parallels with the growth of abortion since it was introduced, and deplored the idea that in certain conditions a life would be declared not worth living.

The ethical argument for assisted dying was taken into new territory in the very next month, when Mr Tony Nicklinson, a sufferer from 'locked-in syndrome' (mentally capable but physically paralysed) obtained clearance to petition the court for permission for a doctor to end his life without being liable to trial for murder. The case was heard in August but the ruling went against him. He refused food thereafter, and died a week later. This was about 'the right to be killed'.

Cost pressures

On the setting up of the welfare state in 1945, it was anticipated that the demand for medical care would diminish as the nation's health improved. In fact, the opposite has happened: a growing and aging population, and advances in treatment and technology, interact to mean that more people live to an age where they contract diseases that are expensive to treat. The result has been funding problems for the NHS. Managers say that they cannot meet all patients' requirements within the financial constraints imposed by the government.

The Care Quality Commission was set up in 2009 but had a difficult start. The chairman resigned after seven months when it was discovered that Basildon Hospital, which had been rated 'good', had filthy wards and a high death rate. It later admitted that it had also made an unforgivable error of judgement in not following up information about the treatment of elderly folk at

Winterborne View. The Department of Health said that the Commission had faced 'strategic difficulties' which challenged public confidence in its role. The exposure of the failings of the Mid-Staffs Trust led one minister to suggest that 'a desire not to face up to the reality of poor care saw institutional secrecy put ahead of patient safety'.

The problem was also aired in July 2011, when the independent Co-operation and Competition Panel published a report saying that NHS managers were having to delay operations (i.e. increase waiting times) to save money, waiting for patients to die or go private. This was described by one observer as 'survival of the wealthiest'.

Politicians continue to claim that the NHS, 'free at the point of delivery' is' the envy of the world' but neither statement is true:

- dentists and opticians charge for their services, and anyone under the age of 60 pays a fee for a prescription;

- the UK is 24th in a list of European countries as regards the doctor to patient ratio (2.7 against 5 in Austria and 4 in Italy). Only Slovenia, Romania and Poland score lower;

- the U.K has the second lowest ratio of beds per 1,000 of population (less than 3, compared with over 6 in France and over 8 in Germany;

- Robert Francis, chairman of the Patients Association and of the inquiry into the Mid-Staffs scandal, said that reports of disturbing, poor and unsafe care remain all too common in the NHS.

I was a non-executive director of an NHS Trust for a total of eight years, but failed entirely to get senior executives in the Trust (or the various layers of bureaucracy above them) to admit that, given finite resources and rapidly increasing demand, some form of rationing needed to be consciously and openly adopted.

Early in 2014, it was reported that the National Institute for Health and Care Excellence ('NICE') were reviewing the criteria used to decide whether or not to license drugs. Specifically, the draft proposals called for the inclusion of a consideration of the value to society of the patient. Predictably, this drew howls of protest, as the inference is that it would be the weaker members of society – the elderly and the mentally or physically disabled - who would be denied treatment. Comparisons were made with policies adopted by the Third Reich.

10. Education – a force for polarisation

Secondary

The coming into operation of the 1944 Education Act revolutionised secondary education. The bill had been guided through by 'Rab' Butler, Francis and Louisa Galton's great nephew, and was designed with social as well as academic objectives in mind. It made *secondary* education available to all, free of charge, and adopted a tripartite approach: grammar, secondary modern and technical, based on selection by examinations (essentially intelligence tests – Galton would have approved) at the age of 11. The outcome was a move towards a more meritocratic approach.

It should be noted that many observers have argued that intelligence as such can't be measured: what such tests measure is the ability to perform well in intelligence tests. However, the consensus among psychologists today seems to be that what they measure is something which – in the light of subsequent achievements - correlates very well with intelligence. Thank Galton for the concept of correlation.

In the event, the idea of technical schools failed to gain traction, and the situation was reached where about 20% of state pupils attended grammar schools, and about 80% secondary modern. The grammar schools did all that was expected of them, in that they offered the best academic education to the brightest children, whatever their background. Their pursuit of excellence - rooted in discipline, respect and competition - was designed to bring out the best in each child, recognising that they were different, one from another. Pupils were constantly reminded that they represented, and had to be a credit to, their schools. In terms of passes gained in the new General Certificate of Education

('GCE') grammar schools were very successful, and it is notable that they provided five consecutive U. K. Prime Ministers (Ted Heath, Harold Wilson, Jim Callaghan, Margaret Thatcher and John Major) but, since 1997, only privately educated men have held the post.

The grammar schools also proved to be powerful engines of social mobility, but brought about a form of polarisation – rooted in intelligence as measured at age 11 - as their pupils tended to meet one another, marry, and have children of grammar school ability (whether inherited, encouraged or tutored) in what amounted, for them at least, to a virtuous circle. Moreover, the better teachers gravitated towards the grammar schools, with the result that opportunities open to secondary modern pupils were severely restricted. Only a small percentage of them sat, let alone passed, any GCE examinations. The prevailing power distribution moved towards something like 20% of children getting 80% of examination successes: the ubiquitous Pareto 'rule'.

But there was a problem, in that the 80% of youngsters who were not admitted to grammar schools were referred to as having *failed*, which many people felt was undesirable, especially at such an early age. A powerful anti-selection lobby began to form, which:

- in general, opposed meritocracy, intelligence tests and competition of any kind. Their mantra was that 'either none or all should have prizes';

- in particular, argued that it was unfair that brighter children should be allowed to outpace the less able ones and, consequently, be better placed as regards qualifications, university access and jobs.

Following the election of a Labour government in 1964, opponents of selection had gained the upper hand, and local authorities were instructed to plan for conversion to a unitary comprehensive system (a step which was to be described by Tony Blair in his memoirs as 'academic vandalism'). This would be accompanied by a new examination, the Certificate of Secondary Education ('CSE') alongside (but at a lower standard than) the GCE. Over a thousand grammar schools were lost over the next few years, though some have managed to survive (at the time of writing, there are still 164 in England). A significant number converted to fee-paying status, which made sense given the increased demand arising from the widespread fear that the comprehensive programme would reduce the quality of state education.

Even where a town went completely over to comprehensives, however, it did not end divisions because, inevitably, schools in some neighbourhoods were seen to be more successful than others, in terms of examination results. This led to a clustering of brighter children, better teachers, and higher house prices (making it more difficult for the children of poorer parents to get places) and therefore tending to recreate a polarisation based on wealth. Remember Pareto's theory that an elite will always emerge.

In particular, the top places in primary school league tables have consistently been dominated by faith schools, which are seen as being more successful in terms of both academic and social skills. Unsurprisingly, church attendance in areas which have oversubscribed faith schools is very strong (against the national trend which is one of decline). Moreover, complex entry rules are said to favour middle class parents who have the time and ability to get involved in activities. Opponents say that this amounts to covert selection, and that the schools should be ordered to be more socially inclusive, i.e. take in less able children. The argument is

124

that they are harming the neighbouring schools, by attracting the better calibre students – better being seen as the enemy of best.

From 1988 onwards, the GCE and CSE examinations were combined into a 'one test fits all' General Certificate of Secondary Education ('GCSE'). When it became obvious that standards were deteriorating, central government imposed various performance measures on schools, notably league tables showing the percentage of pupils gaining GCSE grades A, B or C. In line with the law of unintended (though not unpredictable) consequences, this prompted schools to 'game the system'. Typical tactics were to:

- concentrate on helping pupils heading for a D to become C, whilst ignoring the ones heading for A's or B's ('not too dull, not too bright, being a gamma is just right');

- enter brighter pupils for GCSE's a year early, confident of their achieving at least a C, thereby freeing up resources to concentrate even more on the natural D's;

- discourage students from taking difficult subjects like Mathematics, Science and Languages, and encourage them to take easier ones instead, so as to enhance the average score (whereas the private and selective schools continued to major on the subjects valued by the top universities). This was the main reason, according to outgoing Director of Fair Access, Sir Martin Harris, in July 2012, for the skewed admissions to universities;

- choose between the five examination boards on the basis of whose questions were easiest to answer (described by the Education Select Committee of the House of Commons as a 'race to the bottom' as the boards competed for market share);

125

- teach to the test rather than the entire subject, helped by buying books endorsed by the examiners, and attending seminars designed by them, which offered guidance as to forthcoming questions, and the best way to answer them.

The result was that the quality of British state education continued to deteriorate, relative not only to the private sector but also to competing nations. Three comments by senior Labour ministers are illuminating:

- John Prescott opposed Tony Blair's plans for academies on the grounds that 'if they become good schools, the great danger is that everyone will want to go there';

- Ed Balls argued that 'if there are winners, there must be losers';

- but Alan Milburn pointed out that 'birth, not worth, has become more and more a determinant of people's life chances' thereby reducing social mobility.

A partial response was to introduce an A* grade, in an attempt to distinguish the 'best of the best', i.e. really high performers. Then, in 2012, the Coalition government let it be known that it was thinking of going back to the separate GCE / CSE examinations. Critics pointed out that this would usher in a 'two tier' system, which it would - but is that a good or a bad thing? These ideas were spelled out in June 2013, when the Department of Education unveiled a new examination structure for England (the first exams to be sat in 2017) which they said will provide clearer indications of what is required, so as to prevent examiners dumbing down. Coursework assessment is to be banned, in favour of end-of-course exams – a move opposed by the Association of Teachers and Lecturers on the grounds that they would test recall and memory rather than a range of skills. The CBI on the other hand supported

126

the changes as being necessary to end the situation in which many pupils fall behind, while the brightest are not stretched.

As time has gone by, the problem has been accentuated in that the unskilled / semi-skilled jobs, which people with a secondary modern education tended to fill, have been taken over by machines, computers and robots, creating the conditions for the growth of an underclass. The education system needs to adapt but, politically, the situation has remained anti-selection well into this century:

- the Labour Party continues its opposition to academic selection (despite several high-ranking ministers having sent their own children to selective schools);

- Liberal Democratic Party policy is aimed at 'stopping the establishment of new schools which select by ability, aptitude or faith';

- although a significant proportion of Conservative MP's are in favour of selection, party policy does not support it, preferring to focus on 'academies' and 'free schools' which are subject to less control by local authorities – in terms of class sizes, hours, recruitment, curriculum, parental involvement, etc. - but are not allowed to select. Teaching unions do not support the concept, however, describing such schools as analogous to 'hospitals run by patients'.

In 2012, however, a number of grammar schools had laid out plans for expansion – even to the point of using buildings some distance away. Publicity was given, for example, to a campaign by parents in Sevenoaks for a grammar school to be established as a satellite of neighbouring towns' grammar schools, an approach which received outline support from Kent County Council. However, this was overruled in 2013 by the Department of

Education, on the grounds that the proposed school was a new one rather than a satellite (being mixed, as opposed to the sponsors' girls-only status) but the sponsors were given leave to put forward a revised proposal.

Meanwhile, in June 2013, it was reported that grammar school numbers were at their highest level for 35 years, serving 161,000, or one in twenty pupils. The chairman of the 1922 back bench committee commented that this showed that there is huge parental demand for selective education – and that it was time the government freed up the provision of grammar schools where they did not exist.

The Shadow Education Secretary claimed that such ideas amounted to 'the expansion of academic selection by the back door'. This is correct, and prompted many parents to say that what they would really like was selection by the front door: on average, there have been 10 or more applicants for every grammar school place available, and the head of OFSTED has referred to more than a million youngsters being trapped in 'coasting' comprehensives.

On another tack, however, December 2013 saw the chief inspector of schools, Sir Michael Wilshaw:

- advocating a 'fairer distribution of teachers across the country by way of moving the best teachers to the worst performing areas, in order to 'end an unacceptable waste of human potential'. This looks like a magnified version of teachers ignoring the children expected to get A's and B's, so as to concentrate on getting the Ds up to C;

- singling out Norfolk (a county with no grammar schools whatsoever) as a needy area - but the Shadow Education Secretary pointed out that uncontrolled immigration there (heading for agricultural jobs) was a major factor;

- criticising grammar schools for the fact that the majority of their pupils were from middle class backgrounds.

Tertiary

Following the imposition of comprehensive education at the secondary level, the UK government invested heavily in making university education available to a much larger number of young people (albeit largely by enlarging and renaming polytechnics).

Unsurprisingly, however, it led to a crisis of affordability, the government's answer to which was to move towards a 'market' approach, in which more of the universities' income was to stem from tuition fees paid by students, the cap on which was increased, in 2012, to £9,000 per annum for UK applicants. To cover this cost, undergraduates are granted (interest bearing) loans, which are repayable by way of a specific tax on future earnings. Exacerbated by the cost of maintenance, this naturally reinforces the situation where education is at least partially a function of wealth. According to a 2013 report by the Office of National Statistics, inheritance lump sums are diminishing, as the older generation help to fund grandchildren's education rather than letting their money attract inheritance tax. A natural reaction!

Meanwhile, more and more universities have chosen to set their own admission tests. This was because of concerns that A-level results failed to mark out the brightest candidates – a case of 'grade inflation' according to the Schools Minister. On another tack, the newly appointed 'director of fair access' to universities, Professor Les Ebdon told MPs that he would not be afraid to impose 'nuclear' financial penalties if they did not admit a target proportion of students from less well-off families and poorly performing schools on lower grades. His aim, he later said, was to see one poor student to be admitted for every one from the wealthiest 20% of households. His objective is unashamedly a social engineering one, i.e. to widen the social mix of students in our top universities.

Then a report commissioned by the Department of Business, Innovation and Skills argued that it was unfair of employers to give preference to candidates with good degrees from good universities. Given the ultra-competitive global market, it is not surprising to find that employers were not persuaded of that argument. Interestingly, a number of employers – John Lewis is a good example – recruit on the basis of nature (enthusiasm, work ethic, attitude) rather than nurture (skills, they say, can be taught). Sir Francis would be pleased to think his ideas had permeated the psychology of Human Resources Departments.

Around the same time, attention was drawn to the number of places offered by universities, via strategic partners or agents, to overseas (notably Chinese) students at lower grades than British ones. This is understandable, given that universities are expected to act commercially, and fees charged to overseas students are not capped. Notwithstanding the potential of education to be a massive invisible export, however, the Universities Minister criticised the practice, saying – in apparent contradiction of Professor Ebdon - that admitting people with lower grades would slow down their fellow students and harm performance. Some overseas students obviously enhance the university experience but there is clearly a lack of consensus among those in authority as to the relative importance of:

- contributing to the balance of payments;
- being centres of intellectual eminence, feeding a spirit of enquiry and innovation;
- equipping the future workforce with skills necessary to compete globally.

This came to a head in late August 2012 when the London Metropolitan University lost its licence to admit foreign students – on the grounds that many were bogus, in that they had no intention of studying.

The private sector

Meanwhile, given the poor performance of the state sector, private schools continued to flourish but, apart from a few scholarships / bursaries, their pupils are obviously coming from richer families, giving another nudge to wealth-based polarisation (including what some observers see as preventing the downward mobility of the nice but dim or indolent), At the time of writing, the Prime Minister, the Deputy Prime Minister, the Chancellor of the Exchequer and two thirds of the ministers in the coalition government have been privately educated.

Across a wide spectrum of activity, the privately-educated seem to be notably more successful than the state-educated – including not only finance, journalism, legal and professional, but also the arts and sport.

Referring to 'one of the worst statistics in British sport', it was pointed out by Lord Moynihan, the chairman of the British Olympic Association, that, although privately educated people represent only 7% of the UK population, they accounted for over half of the medals won by British athletes in Beijing in 2008, which he described as 'wholly unacceptable'. Notwithstanding the fact that the corresponding ratio at London 2012 was slightly better, he called for an overhaul of state education system to raise standards of school sport so that the other 93% had the same opportunity as the 7%.

Sir Peter Lampl of the Sutton Trust said that the mismatch was not surprising, as pupils at private schools benefit from ample time set aside for sport, coupled with investment in facilities and coaching – whereas in state run schools it was not a priority. This naturally led to appeals for the government to do something, pointing out some of the problems:

- the sale of 10,000 playing fields:

- the School Teachers Pay and Conditions Act of 1991 which (following various strikes and work to rule campaigns by teachers) restricted their after-school duties;

- the opposition to competition in principle, i.e. not wanting to segregate children into winners and losers, as this damages their self-esteem. Olympic gold medal winner Jessica Ennis expressed the opposite view, i.e. that youngsters need to learn that competition is positive.

As Francis Galton would remind us, however, correlation does not necessarily mean cause and effect. Yes, the private schools have better facilities and equipment, encourage aspiration, and provide more extra-curricular activities but, he would suggest, it may be that their students are more capable anyway, have more self-confidence to get involved, and / or have more indulging parents.

In June 2013, entrepreneur James Caan was appointed as the government's 'social mobility tsar' but surprised people with his first utterances being advice to middle class parents not to help their children's careers: it would be better for them to make their own way. But would that not mean that they would be even more successful, making it more difficult for others? Deputy Prime Minister Nick Clegg chose to distance himself from Mr Caan's views.

Meanwhile, announcing the setting up of an inquiry into the gulf between rich and poor children in British Schools, Sir Michael Wilshaw referred to an anti-school culture amongst hundreds of thousands of children. White British boys eligible for free school meals perform worse than any other group except gypsies and travellers, which he put down to their being surrounded by generations of worklessness after the demise of traditional industries. Teachers were having to act as surrogate parents, including explaining the difference between right and wrong.

Interpretation

In short, the debate remains unsettled, in that it is possible to recognise three different views, as follows.

- The first harks back to Vilfredo Pareto's observation, namely that a gulf between rich and poor is a characteristic of human society, and interference is unlikely to achieve anything. He would not have any problem with the fact that the better off are still able to pay for the best education for their children.

- The second conforms to Francis Galton's idea that the more intelligent members of the population should be helped to form communities, in which eminence would thrive. The grammar schools had this effect, in both academic and social terms, and he would undoubtedly be in the camp pleading for their rehabilitation and expansion.

- Thirdly is the view of the opponents of selection, who challenge not the record of the grammar schools, but the desirability of the results. They genuinely believe that a meritocracy is undesirable because it is unfair, and that the chosen approach should aim to achieve equality of outcome (even if this means levelling down).

Giving the Reith lectures in 2012, Professor Niall Ferguson lent his support to the ideas mooted by Milton Friedman that government investment in education should be directed to the customer by way of vouchers, enabling parents to choose to which school to send their children (rather than the producers, i.e. schools and highly unionised teachers).

11. Population, race and migration

World population

When Francis Galton died in 1911, the world population was less than 2 billion. Fifty years on, coincident with the founding by Sir Julian Huxley and others, of the World Wildlife Fund (with the aim of identifying the causes of losses of charismatic species, and devising ways of slowing them down if not stopping them) it had doubled, to around 3.5 billion.

In introducing his RSA president's lecture in the spring of 2011, Sir David Attenborough noted that, another fifty years on, the world population had more than doubled again to over 7 billion, increasing the demand for space to live, to produce food and to build amenities etc. The only way that demand could be met had been at the expense of the natural world. Simultaneously, industrialisation had changed the chemical constitution of the atmosphere, polluted and acidified the oceans, and caused the collapse of fish stocks, the loss of rainforests, and the acceleration of climate change.

In Sir David's view, although developments in science and technology had postponed the predicted impact, Malthus was fundamentally right: there cannot be more people on earth than can be fed, as evidenced by frequent Ethiopian famines: a clear case of too many people (the population there having doubled in the last 25 years, to over 80 million) on a finite amount of land. A 'perfect storm' embracing population growth, climate change, and the passing of peak oil production was foreseeable, to the point that there was no major problem facing our planet that would not be easier to solve if there were fewer people on it, and no problem that was not becoming harder – and ultimately impossible - to solve with ever more.

135

However, he drew attention to what he called a 'bizarre taboo' as regards talking about overpopulation. If the consequence was not to be a significant increase in the death rate (by way of famine, disease, or wars fought over water or energy) there was a need for a population policy. Interviewed in January 2012, he argued that the human race was threatening its own and other species' existence by exhausting the world's resources. Either we limit population growth, he said, or the natural world will do it for us. Returning to the subject in September 2013, he made the point that we had chosen to put a halt to natural selection, and stressed the need for people to be persuaded that it is irresponsible to have large families.

In aggregate, humanity is increasingly better fed, and is achieving greater life expectancy, thanks largely to medical and nutritional advances. The number of children per mother is reducing significantly as a result of better education, the availability of contraceptives, prompting a delay in starting a family so as to pursue a career. Above a certain level of prosperity, every society has experienced a demographic transition to a lower birth rate. But this does affect the mix of a given population, there being a strong *inverse* correlation between the education of women and the size of families - the exact opposite of what Plato, Malthus and Galton recommended.

Growth is currently most evident in the poorer areas – notably Africa and the Indian subcontinent. As it was at the time of Malthus, humanitarianism has the effect of shifting, or even exacerbating, the problem in the long term, as with:

- the UK government's foreign aid policy, such as the commitment in June 2011 to donate £800 million to the Global Alliance campaign for vaccines and immunization against pneumonia and diarrhea, which was predicted to save 4 million lives. Opponents pointed out that the resulting increase in population would aggravate poverty; if such a sum of money was available (in fact, it is being borrowed) would contraception not be a better use for it?

- the pleas of charities to donate £x per month to help save lives, e.g. '2,000 children a day die every day because they lack safe water and sanitation'. Research at the University of Bristol found that such help did improve water supplies in the villages, and reduced infant mortality, but that the resulting increased population put pressure on food supplies, meaning more moved to the urban slums to find work.

The Bill and Melinda Gates foundation, on the other hand, does donate billions to efforts to provide safe contraception to millions of women in developing countries. Melinda Gates pointed out that unwanted and unplanned pregnancies were causing hundreds of thousands of girls to die in pregnancy, and millions of children to die in the first year of their lives.

UK population

Currently, the United Kingdom population is showing the highest rate of growth in Europe, and the Office for National Statistics ('ONS') expects it to continue to increase by half a million a year for the next fifteen years, taking it to 80 million. Three contributory pressures have been identified.

The first is an increased birth rate. Currently running at over 800,000 births per annum, the highest for over thirty years, this puts extra pressure on midwifery services etc. A report by the ONS indicated that a major factor was the increase in the number of foreign born women, who displayed a higher than average fertility (over 25% of those births are to mothers born outside the UK).

The second is increased longevity, which is having a significant effect on the costs of health and welfare borne by the government, as highlighted in a report by the Social Mobility Commission (chaired by Alan Milburn, the former Labour Health Secretary). This blamed the practice of universal benefits, whereby all elderly people were entitled to such benefits as bus passes, winter fuel allowances, and free television licences. He urged the removal of such benefits from the better off, thereby ensuring that they suffered a 'fairer share' of the pain of government cuts.

As the total population increases, so does its average age, as was highlighted in a debate in the House of Lords in which several peers warned that ministers were failing to prepare public services to deal with the pressures brought on by a totally predictable increase in the proportion of elderly people in the population. Others have warned of the danger of inter-generational conflict, given that, though wages and salaries have fallen in real terms, many of the elderly are living on final salary pensions in homes that have soared in value. Having worked hard, paid taxes and saved, however, and now helping their grandchildren with the increased cost of university education, they expect a dignified old age. Others, meanwhile, are struggling to get by on savings that have been reduced in value by successive government economic policies.

The third is immigration, which will be dealt with later in this chapter.

Race

Charles Darwin and Francis Galton disagreed about race: the former saw only one human species, but the latter recognised differences between races – and the debate continues to this day.

On Darwin's side is the fact that mating is possible across the whole of the human population. Medically, however, there are significant differences, typified by the fact that, if Asians need bone marrow transplants, the only possible matches are fellow Asians.

Arthur Jensen (1923 – 2012) caused controversy in 1969, when he published the results of research into intelligence. This showed that, though 'associative learning ability' (memorising facts) was spread evenly, 'conceptual learning ability' (problem solving) varied across the races. His suggestion that this should be reflected in the tailoring of education saw him branded as a racist.

The London 2012 Olympics brought the debate to a wider public. Note, for example, how black athletes dominate running events, especially at the shorter distances: of the 82 fastest sprinters in the world, 81 are black. Are black people inherently better runners than white – or has success bred success in that today's black youngsters see what can be achieved and will train assiduously? In other words, is the difference explained by nature or nurture?

Another feature of the Olympics was the cult of nationalism: many of the 'Team GB' medal winners said they could not have done it without the partisan support of the home crowd. Hardly in tune with the Olympic spirit! On a sadder note, football has been dogged by out-and-out racism, with some supporters indulging in offensive barracking, hissing, Hitler salutes, monkey gestures and chants, and the throwing of bananas - and frequent racial abuse by players, some reaching the courts.

Increased nationalism is also evidenced by the growth in the number of independent countries: from 89 in 1945 to 195 in 2013. Many of the splits have been as a result of the wealthier part wishing to separate itself from the poorer.

Migration

Anyone versed in the physical sciences will be aware of the laws of thermodynamics – which actually have wider application than their name might suggest. In particular, the second law highlights the tendency for all natural systems to have a 'preferred direction of travel'. Heat flows from areas of high temperature to areas of low temperature, for example, and air moves from areas of high pressure to areas of low pressure, causing winds.

Adopting the early social scientists path of attempting to 'Newtonise' their specialism, we might observe some similarity as regards the movement of people. Migration, from one area of the country to another, has always been a factor in the development of the British economy, as labour has moved from areas where demand was weak and wages therefore relatively low, to ones where demand was strong and hence wages high.

I am the product of such a process: as Bradford on Avon's woollen trade declined in the nineteenth century, for example, my great-grandfather Allen, in common with many others, moved himself and his family from Wiltshire to the outskirts of Birmingham, to find work in the iron and steel industry. My other great-grandfathers hailed from Shropshire, Nottinghamshire and Herefordshire, all moving as part of the exodus from the land. Many readers will no doubt have similar ancestry.

According to Dr Malcolm Dick, writing in the Birmingham University magazine *History West Midlands*, it tends to be the more enterprising people who are motivated to seek new opportunities elsewhere. He was focusing on migration within the United Kingdom, but the same is likely to apply to migration as between countries. It has similar origins, as the supply of labour adapts to the demand, but it is accompanied by difficulties on account of colour, religion and culture. We can add language to that list, though because English is such a popular second language, English-speaking countries are especially popular destinations. As it happens, however, immigration into the British Isles in the nine hundred years to 1950 is reckoned to have been no more than a quarter of a million, mainly Jews and Huguenots.

Immigration into the United Kingdom

The situation in the U.K. was to change with the passing of the 1948 Nationality Act, which gave 800 million Commonwealth citizens the right to live in Britain. This was a consequence of the coming together of two pressures:

- political, amounting to a sense of gratitude and responsibility to the people of countries that had fought valiantly alongside the Allies in the Second World War;

- economic, in the form of a shortage of unskilled labour as the British economy recovered from the ravages of that war. Employers in the area around Birmingham, among others, actively sought to recruit from the West Indies.

Later that year, the well-publicised *Empire Windrush* (formerly a cruise ship reserved for Nazi elite) arrived at Tilbury docks from Jamaica, with 493 passengers seeking a new life in Great Britain.

The demographic shockwaves which that Act created took a while to impress themselves on public consciousness, the first major event being the Notting Hill riots in 1958. By the time of the 1964 general election, however, the scale was recognised, especially around Birmingham: Peter Griffiths (1928 – 2013) won Smethwick (Sir Oswald Moseley's former constituency, it will be recalled) for the Conservatives, ousting the Foreign Secretary designate, Patrick Gordon Walker. According to Labour party members, Griffiths' supporters had been in the habit of chanting 'If you want a nigger for a neighbour, vote Liberal or Labour'. On his arrival at the House of Commons, Prime Minister Harold Wilson branded him a 'parliamentary leper' – but he was later to represent Portsmouth North for 18 years.

Perhaps the most memorable oration on the subject was Enoch Powell's address to a Conservative Association meeting in what was then the Midland Hotel in Birmingham in April 1968, in which he argued that the supreme function of statesmanship was to provide against preventable evils, but acknowledged that such evils were difficult to demonstrate until they have actually occurred. He identified the risk that people are disposed to mistake the act of predicting troubles for causing – and even desiring – them.

That was a precursor to talking about a problem which, in his view, was being played down by political leaders and the media, namely the growth of the immigrant population, leading to undesirable pressures on public services and the infrastructure. He also warned of the danger of a fragmentation of society on account of 'communalism', i.e. immigrants seeking not to integrate but to foster racial and religious differences. His quantification of the likely growth – recognising higher birth rates amongst immigrants as well as new arrivals, including dependants - proved to be remarkably accurate. By 1981, for instance, immigrants accounted for more than 50% of the population of the Birmingham ward in which Francis Galton had been born – Sparkbrook and Sparkhill. It should be noted, however, that the local authority's policy on housing (requiring five years' residence in Birmingham, to be eligible for tenancies of the new council houses being built in the suburbs) contributed to the concentration of immigrants in the inner city.

Powell restated the official Conservative policy at the time, namely the restriction of immigration, coupled with repatriation – but treating those here with equality before the law. However, his closing remarks 'As I look ahead, I am filled with foreboding; like the Romans, I seem to see the River Tiber foaming with much blood' upset leading Tories (especially Ted Heath, Quintin Hogg and Ian McLeod) with the consequence that he was dismissed from the shadow cabinet. Opinion polls at the time showed three quarters of the population agreed with Powell, and rated him the most popular politician in the country. Thirty years later, Heath admitted that Powell's views on the economic burden of immigration had been 'not without prescience'. Faint praise!

The next notable eruption came in 1984 when Bradford headmaster Ray Honeyford, whose school was 90% Muslim, went public with his concerns. He was worried by the growing number of Asians who wanted to maintain the culture of the Indian subcontinent within a framework of British social and political privilege, but knew little of the host culture, e.g. civilised discourse, democracy, the rule of law and respect for women. He disagreed with local authority policy which, he said:

- allowed children months of absence to 'go home' to Pakistan on the grounds that it was appropriate to their culture;

- celebrated linguistic diversity leading to linguistic confusion;

- used the word 'racism' as a slogan to discourage constructive thought;

- condoned a situation which was failing indigenous children.

In short, he was challenging what Powell had called communalism, but has since come to be known as separatism, or national multiculturalism, arguing that it was also doing a

143

disservice to immigrant children who were thereby denied the benefits of full integration into British society. However, such was the backlash that he felt obliged to take early retirement.

A further iteration of the problem arose from the open door policy of the New Labour government from 1997 onwards (and the subsequent decision not to restrict immigration from Eastern Europe). The policy, summed up by Home Secretary David Blunkett in terms of there being 'no obvious upper limit to legal immigration', again had both economic and political roots:

- in the short term, to help the economy to grow and to fund the costs associated with an increasingly elderly population; and

- in the longer term, to develop an enriched multicultural experience which would be valuable given the rapid rate of globalisation.

Over the 13 years of New Labour governments, there was a net immigration of over 4 million to the U.K. (precision being impossible on account of the suspicion that there had been large numbers of illegal entrants) causing two main concerns. Firstly, the growth of the economy was short lived, but immigration continued at a rapid rate, creating enormous pressures, identified in a Home Office report as follows.

- overcrowding, leading to pest control issues;

- increased social misbehaviour and community tensions;

- increased demand on local services and hence a stretching of resources;

- greater incidence of serious diseases and mental health problems;

- a higher birth rate, increasing demand for midwifery, maternity and health visiting;

- multilingualism, causing delays and extra costs.

By 2013, there were over 2.6 million foreign citizens working in the United Kingdom (of the same order as the number of indigenous unemployed) and, according to the Department of Education, there were over a million schoolchildren in England who did not speak English at home. In primary education, this averaged 20% across the country as a whole but, in some boroughs in London, it was above 70%. 108 different languages are spoken in Birmingham's schools and pupils at the English Martyrs School in Galton's Sparkhill speak no less than 31 different languages at home.

Secondly, the objective was never integration: ethnic identity continued to be seen as more important than adaptation to the host culture, leading to the development of ghettos. This had a profound effect on public opinion and, though many Labour seats in the 2010 election depended on the immigrant vote, and outgoing Prime Minister Gordon Brown was overheard during the campaign describing a Labour voter who had asked a genuine question about immigration as a 'bigoted woman', in public he promised to ensure 'British jobs for British workers'. One wonders how he would have done that, given European Union regulations.

Commenting on riots which had taken place in several cities in 2011, historian David Starkey described what he called an inescapable and painful conclusion, namely that the core of the rioters comprised an already existing criminal class, which was disproportionately black. Unsurprisingly, he was accused of racism but, in actual fact, he focused on a particular sort of culture: 'destructive, nihilistic, anti-education, Jafaican patois, and rap and gangsta music, the lyrics of which glorify violence.' A few months later, Adolph Cameron, head of the Jamaican Teachers' Association echoed those thoughts, and added that to speak in Standard English was seen by such boys as 'a woman's activity' not consistent with their notion of masculinity.

The Conservative / Liberal coalition that had been elected in 2010 said that they planned to reduce net immigration from hundreds of thousands to tens of thousands by 2015. As of 2013, however, it was still running at over 200,000 p.a. (526,000 immigrants minus 314,000 emigrants), and 1 in 4 children starting school in the autumn of that year had a foreign born mother. At this stage, even those in the socialist camp began to adjust their thinking. In June 2012, Ed Milliband, leader of the Labour Party, admitted that Eastern European immigration had been much higher than his party had predicted (700,000 against 'up to 15,000'); and that it was not racist to talk about it. Of course it wasn't: European immigrants, being white, are not seen as belonging to a foreign race. We should thank the European Community for serving to separate the question of immigration from racism.

In November 2012, the government's planning minister, Nick Boles, said that we need to increase the amount of land which is built on by a third. He argued that people who oppose development are denying adequate space for their children and grandchildren. The built environment, he said, can be more beautiful than nature. Unfortunately, his remarks coincided with reports of substantial flooding, much of which related to houses built, with government encouragement, on flood plains. Moreover, the indigenous population sees the problem as being too many people, not too few houses.

Then, in March 2013, David Goodhart (director of the think tank 'Demos') acknowledged that he and fellow liberals had supported the policy of unrestricted immigration, thinking that it would combat what they saw as racism in the U.K. However, from interviews in preparation for his book, *The British Dream*, he realised that mass immigration ('too much, too fast, unmanaged') had had a profoundly adverse effect on British democracy and social cohesion. He singled out the tendency for ethnic minorities to lead segregated lives, in ghettos, a situation that was exacerbated by what Demos called the 'white retreat' from areas dominated by non-whites. In the ten years to 2011, for example, over 600,000 white people had left London and, by then, the remainder constituted the minority. Sir Andrew Green, chairman of Migration Watch, described the situation as 'sleepwalking into segregation'.

Indeed, as highlighted by Nick de Bois, secretary of the 1922 committee of backbench MP's, a total of 3.6 million people had emigrated from the UK in the first decade of the twenty first century, about half of whom were classified as professional / managerial (and only about 3% as retired). He saw this as an exodus of skill and talent that needed to be stemmed. According to the OECD, 1.3 million Britons with university degrees are living abroad – the highest number of any developed country.

In 2013, both the Speaker of the House of Commons (at an event in the parliament in Bucharest) and the Mayor of London (at the Conservative Party Conference) expressed the view that the immigrants from Eastern Europe over recent years had showed more aptitude for, and commitment to, work than did British people. However, we should be concerned that, if it is the more able people who migrate from the poor countries to the rich ones, that actually widens the difference between the two. This force for divergence – typified by the U.K. actively seeking to recruit nurses from Eastern and Southern Europe - in a Community dedicated to convergence, is an excellent example of the law of unintended consequences.

Either way, the views of a substantial proportion of the U. K. electorate became clear in the Eastleigh by-election in early 2013, in which the Conservative Party polled fewer votes than the United Kingdom Independence Party ('UKIP') whose members would like to free the United Kingdom from the dictates of the European Union. This was to be repeated on a much larger scale in the elections to the European Parliament in May 2014, when UKIP secured more votes and seats than any other party.

Race revisited

Later in 2013, there was a well-publicised case in which a gang comprising Pakistani Muslims was found to have lured vulnerable young girls into a life as sex slaves. Press reports noted that such activities went on for far too long because police were very wary of being accused of being racist. Trevor Phillips, the former head of the Equality and Human Rights Commission commented that only the criminally deluded would ignore the racial element when addressing the problem of gangs grooming and abusing young girls.

2013 also saw the outbreak of a 'conflict of rights' regarding the wearing of veils by some Muslim women, which many people see as being a visible statement of separateness, and therefore hindering integration. In the space of a few days, it was reported that:

- Birmingham Metropolitan College had been pressured by an 8,000 strong petition into abandoning its policy requiring students not to hide their faces, on the grounds that it discriminated against Muslims as a religious grouping;

- a judge in London insisted that a Muslim defendant (in a case of intimidation) should not hide her face from the jury;

- some Islamic schools insist that female pupils wear veils between home and school;

- the wearing of veils by medical staff had been a controversial issue in a number of hospitals.

On one side of the debate is the view that it is the women's human right to choose what to wear (but, presumably, accept the consequences, e.g. not being allowed into places where veils are inappropriate). On the other, the view expressed by a number of MPs was that the veil is a misogynist imposition, which prevents the women concerned from playing a full part in society, and should therefore be banned.

This was followed in 2014 by the Education watchdog Ofsted putting Park View School in Birmingham into special measures. This was after two special inspections, against the background of an alleged campaign (code name 'Trojan Horse') to 'Islamise' Birmingham's state schools.

Individual cultures strike a balance between competing rights – but, unfortunately, what we have in these instances is a juxtaposition of competing cultures.

12. The current scene

Equal and opposite

Most of Sir Francis Galton's achievements – in exploration, meteorology, fingerprinting etc. – were not at all controversial, though his name is rarely mentioned in those contexts. Similarly with his statistical discoveries: I learned to apply and calculate dispersion, regression and correlation many years ago, as part of my management accountancy studies - but without knowing where they had originated.

So why is it that Galton's name so rarely appears in credits for the above achievements, even in his home city? Why does the large scale permanent 'History of Birmingham' exhibition in the city's main museum make no reference to him? How is it that the people in the city's information offices have never heard of him? The answer to all of these questions is that his reputation has been so tainted by association with what the Fabians, Fascists, and especially the Nazis, said and did in the name of eugenics, as to render him *persona non grata.*

Galton's reputation is not the only issue here. Beyond that, there are so many current issues, as is clear from chapters 8 – 11, in which the principles of eugenics *as propagated by Galton himself* would be a relevant input. Unfortunately, the word 'eugenics' is taboo because so many people assume that it is synonymous with Nazi atrocities – which undoubtedly amounted to a catastrophic collapse of humanitarian values.

In an attempt to deal with these issues, let us begin by recognising that Galton's eugenics sprang out of his work on heredity. His fundamental assertion – that people are not born equal - ran into considerable opposition at the time, notably from religious fundamentalists. As the years have gone by, however, and our knowledge of genetics has blossomed, disagreement has faded. It is now incontestable that some people are naturally more intelligent, and / or have a stronger work ethic etc., than others, and therefore will be more successful. Society will consequently display an inequality of eminence and potentially, therefore, wealth and income. The question is whether this should be encouraged, accepted or prevented.

Galton was in the 'encouragement' camp, arguing that eminence should first of all be identified, and then reinforced through the provision of financial and other forms of support. He hoped that such a 'meritocratic' approach would encourage the eminent to breed faster than the less eminent (who were to be discouraged therefrom) thereby improving the average and aggregate quality of the population over the long term. He applied these ideas both within individual races, and as between the races that constitute the human species.

If we observe the contemporary scene, however, we see little evidence of these ideas in practice. Indeed, as in Galton's time, social and political pressures are all pulling in the opposite direction. There is, for example, an inverse correlation between wealth and family size: it is the poorer families in the U.K., and the poorer populations across the world, who are having the most children – and being subsidised through the tax system or charity. This situation arises from a viewpoint that is diametrically opposed to that of Galton (and Plato, and Malthus) namely that inequality and meritocracy are socially unacceptable and therefore need to be mitigated, if not extinguished.

In an economic context, this is the argument that is used to justify taking money away from the better off by way of taxes, and giving it (minus a substantial administration cost) to the less well off in the form of benefits or foreign aid. The technical term is 'redistribution' but, unfortunately, it tends to have the effect of reducing aggregate wealth creation, by removing incentives, and creating disincentives. Galton would observe another inverse correlation here: the greater the equality, the lower the overall achievement.

This levelling down is a long way from the thinking of the early Fabians who, alongside their support for eugenics, plotted the gradual adoption of a form of socialism in which the masses were to be led by an elite. The Beveridge report, it will be recalled, advocated that benefits be seen as safety nets, and be dependent on contributions, which were to be 'flat rate', i.e. the same for everyone, irrespective of means. The Fabians abhorred the concept of an 'entitlement society'. How, then, did we reach the point where the dominant characteristic of our society is a sustained emphasis on seeking to benefit the masses at the expense of the elite? Galton's work on averages may hold a clue, along the following lines.

- The median figure for wealth, income, etc. will always fall short of the corresponding weighted arithmetic mean.
- Hence, the number of people below that arithmetic mean will always constitute a majority of the population. David Lloyd George understood this, declaring his intention to 'bring the magic of averages to the rescue of the millions'.
- Politicians seeking office will naturally bend towards doing what they think will please the majority of the population. This amounts to following rather than leading, and the circle is completed by voters who keep voting for politicians who promise them more benefits but lower taxation.

Hence a 'regression to the mediocre' is almost assured.

Similarly, in an education context, the move to a 'comprehensive' approach owed much to the persistence of the pre-Galton belief that the mind was an open book, such that nurture could outweigh nature. In the event, it has deprived many brighter children of the opportunity to proceed at a pace appropriate to them, as teachers have had to devote more time and effort to the less bright (not least by way of attempts to impose discipline on those born without the motivation to learn). Again, this has amounted to a levelling down, as a consequence of which the gap between the achievements of state schools and private schools has widened, and the U.K. has slipped down the international league table for educational success. Perversely, the official reaction has been to put even more (costly) resource into nurture, and to turn a blind eye to nature.

Alongside the above, the welfare state is clearly unaffordable: the government continues to spend hundreds of millions of pounds per annum more than it receives. At the time of writing, its accumulated borrowings amount to around £1.4 trillion - that's £20,000 for every man, woman and child in the Kingdom – as well as which it has massive unfunded liabilities. Given the steady improvement in longevity, without a change in policy, this state of affairs will continue to deteriorate: government receipts are projected to fall significantly short of expenditure under current fiscal policies. In the spring of 2014, the Institute of Economic Affairs predicted 'crippling' tax rises and spending cuts – but acknowledged that these would choke off economic growth. The underlying problem, they explained, was that successive governments had made promises they could not honour from contemporary receipts: 'the electorate is grazing a fiscal common at the expense of future generations'. In Galton's day, this would have been seen as unethical if not immoral; today, the potential for intergenerational conflict is clear.

Meanwhile, the need for charity has not faded away as Clement Attlee asserted it would, but has expanded. There are currently over 150,000 charities in the United Kingdom: vital services such as hospices, the air ambulance and the lifeboat services are all dependent on charity, and we get a couple of fundraisers a month from various worthy causes knocking on our door, asking us to sign up to direct debits.

The fundamental question is how to help without encouraging, as with, for example, the following.

- How do we care for the unmarried mother on the council estate without encouraging her to have more children, or for her friends to follow suit as a career choice?

- How do we care for the starving child in Africa without encouraging its mother to have more children than she can afford to feed?

- How do we help the low-paid without discouraging them from learning a skill?

Time frames

Galton's approach was characteristically long termist, in that he sought improvement 'over several generations' but therein lies the problem. We do not seem to be able to think long term, as evidenced by the following observations.

- The increase in the U.K. population, mainly down to immigration, is seen as a way of solving short term government financial problems (i.e. raising more taxes on income which can go towards funding welfare) notwithstanding the long term effects on the infrastructure. Indeed, the building of houses on flood plains is seen as something quite disconnected from population policy, and owners of properties that are duly flooded are compensated by 'the government', for which read other taxpayers. Meanwhile, multiculturalism has developed to the point where maintaining ethnicity is seen as more important than adapting to the host culture.

- The managers of quoted companies focus on share prices, which correlate with short run profits. Any proposal which would reduce short term profits, even if it benefited future profits by significantly more, would get short shrift. Even worse, the banking crisis came about because senior managers made loans with a high interest rate (enhancing current year profits) but a high risk of future default (reducing profits in some future year) without fear of retribution – a situation referred to as 'moral hazard'.

- Within large multi-product businesses, it is difficult to avoid cross-subsidisation. The best resources are often found to be associated with the worst products, economically speaking; the better products are often forced to make more profit than is good for long term health; and so on. All this amounts to money flowing out of profitable products into unprofitable ones. In this context, think of Sir Michael Wilshaw's desire to send the best teachers to the worst schools.

- The unemployed focus on the net increment to current income, i.e. the excess of the starting wage over the benefits foregone, lacking the work ethic and foresight to see that the job contains the prospect of higher income in the future.

- On a larger scale, moral hazard in the Eurozone has meant that the profligate south (taking on borrowings which they could not service or repay) has had to be bailed out by the disciplined north (following the 'economic superiority' strategy criticised by Hitler).

- Climate change is a good example of the 'prisoner's dilemma in that individual countries do not see a benefit in unilateral greening, e.g. higher energy taxes are seen as impeding economic growth. Their inability to co-operate means that we all lose.

The amazing thing (to all but those who follow Vilfredo Pareto's thinking) is that, notwithstanding the sustained application of this populist form of socialism, inequality has not been eliminated. Witness the Pope's New Year message in 2013, in which he referred to growing inequality, which he linked to 'the prevalence of a selfish and individualistic mind-set which also finds expression in unregulated capitalism', a situation in line with Adam Smith's predictions, and reminiscent of the warnings of both Mussolini and Hitler.

In the U.K., a contributory factor was the government's response to the financial crisis, i.e. keeping real interest rates below zero. This was a deliberate strategy aimed at discouraging new capital formation (saving and investment for the future) in order to boost current consumption and keep borrowers afloat. Perversely, it has boosted existing capital values – meaning that the gap between rich and poor has actually grown. Whether this was an intended or unintended consequence is a moot point.

Some would argue that we should accept that the human race is basically selfish, and adapt our policies accordingly, rather than hoping that we can somehow become altruistic. However, it is worth observing from game theory that players with a short timeframe see the game as a zero sum one, and are more likely to 'betray' one another. Conversely, those with a longer time frame, are more likely to see it as a win-win one, and are more likely to 'co-operate' with one another.

Religion

We can't expect politicians to lead a move towards a situation in which the role of the state is drastically reduced. Neither will they work to give the long term more attention: their horizon is no further away than the next election. But what should be the philosophy that enables us to navigate between the extremes of inhuman fascism and unaffordable populism? Is there a genuine and feasible third way?

A good starting point might be to agree that one of the most depressing sentences in the English language is: 'The government should do something about it'. Though such a view is still prevalent, we can be encouraged by the observation of Justin Welby, the Archbishop of Canterbury on taking office in February 2013 that, thanks to the financial crisis, the state has run out of the capacity to do the things that it has taken over since 1945. This provided an opportunity for charities and the Church, he said.

After all, religion is nothing if not long termist. Matthew Arnold (1822 – 1888) suggested that religion is 'motivated ethics', or 'morality touched by emotion' and shared Galton's view that it provides an agency which encourages action which is right for the race, being in harmony with the perceived underlying plan for the universe.

It is worth remembering that, in days gone by, the church was active in channelling funds from the fortunate to the unfortunate, so as to fund education, welfare and the like. However, such activity atrophied in the face of the policies we saw espoused by Clement Attlee, to the effect that charity should not be at the whim of the rich, but funded by confiscating private wealth and distributed by a state bureaucracy.

A question of scale

Concomitant with the drift to the left has been an increase in the scale of political set-ups, and, indeed, the two trends seem to be mutually reinforcing. It would, for example, take a particular form of altruism for those in authority to actively reduce the role of the state, and hence their job opportunities. We now have the answers to the questions asked in the Cadbury's booklet, listed in chapter 8, and they do not provide any comfort at all:

- people do take for granted the various benefits and services provided by the state;

- the way that the national insurance scheme has been modified does impede the incentive to work hard;

- progressive taxation does penalize hard work;

- state monopolies do not have a good history as regards productivity and value for money;

- the exchange rate has continued to deteriorate (down 60% against the dollar since 1945) reflecting balance of payments deficits and greater inflation than other countries.

This prompts me to draw on my experience in industry and, in particular, what I have identified as 'managerial megatrends'. For most of the twentieth century, stability was regarded as normal: the assumption was that tomorrow would be very much like yesterday. However, towards the end of that century, and into this – thanks to scientific and technological developments, globalisation etc. - the pace of change picked up, such that the safest assumption now is that tomorrow will be different. As a consequence, the predominant features of management practice have themselves experienced a revolution, as follows.

- The old model majored on the short termist tactical level of control, which is concerned with *how* to do what it is assumed the business will always do, e.g. how high a selling price to charge, how much stock to carry. The new model, on the other hand, majors on the long termist strategic level, which is concerned with *what* the business does: the markets it serves, the products it offers, the facilities it uses.

- The old model was a supply sided one, emphasising the products (be they goods or services) that the business offered – they did not welcome customers who wanted something different. As competition - especially international competition – has increased, this has led to a shrinking of such businesses. So, the new model is a demand sided one, emphasising what would delight the customer, and requiring flexibility of supply.

- The old model was very much a top down one, with all key decisions being made at the centre of the organisation. However, it gradually dawned that such an approach was simply not fast enough on its feet to adapt to changing customer requirements, new ways of working, or competitors' initiatives. The new model, therefore, seeks to push authority out to those closest to the action, especially those close to the customers.

- The old model was very functionalist, the most senior positions being defined in terms of responsibility for production, sales, distribution etc. This inevitably led to sub-optimisation: production directors tended to oppose variety and customisation, for example, because they had an adverse effect on reported productivity and efficiency. The new model, therefore, is based on generalism, with all managers alert to what is best for the organisation as a whole.

- The control mechanism of the old model can be summarised in the expression 'command and compliance', in which underlings were expected to conform to handed-down decisions. The control mechanism of the new model, meanwhile, can be summarised in the expression 'trust and commitment' in which objectives are communicated and decisions delegated.

- The old model, not surprisingly, was characterised by conflict: between functions within the business, between capital and labour, and even between the business and its suppliers and customers. These days, however, successful businesses are characterised by collaboration, seeing that, in the long term, the interests of the various stakeholders can be harmonised.

- The old model was a left-brain one, attaching importance to such things as measurement, analysis, knowledge and repetition – attributes associated with stability. The new model is a right-brain one and, being accepting of volatility, attaches importance to such things as assessment, synthesis, imagination and innovation.

Importantly, however, it is clear that large organisations (notably government departments and quoted companies) find it extremely difficult, if not impossible, to make the transition from the old to the new. Their top managers cannot imagine how it is possible to devolve authority without losing control, or how a rigid plan actually impedes good strategic management. Smaller organisations (notably owner-managed businesses) are in their element in today's conditions, to the point that they are recognised as the backbone of a growing economy.

In short, the successful organisations are characterised by a drift to the right, not only in terms of the predominant side of the brain, but also in terms of the political spectrum as outlined in chapter 6. What does this mean for Galton's *vox populi*? Interestingly, recent research by Princeton University has shown that decision accuracy is not a simple function of group size. It increases up to a point, but then decreases – a bit like the normal curve, we might say.

The important thing is that these businesses will experiment with different approaches as regards products, markets, facilities, and ways of working. Some of them will succeed, enabling the businesses to grow; others will fail, causing them to shrink. Business is a competitive struggle for existence, in which those best fitted for the prevailing environment will be the ones to survive, and enhance the economy as a whole. This is what gives economics value as an analogy for the many of the topics in this book.

Back to the future

When one looks at the U.K. government's borrowings, in excess of a trillion pounds, it is difficult to avoid the inference that the experiment with populist socialism has failed not just the nation as a whole, but even the section thereof that in theory it was meant to benefit. Politicians of all hues have consistently led us down the wrong path, and we are suffering the consequences.

So, let us set aside the story from the early Fabians onwards, and look again at the thinking of the Georgian and Victorian polymaths we saw in chapters 1 to 5. The nation made its greatest progress in those days of laissez-faire and minimal government interference. Yes, the industrialists did well in terms of personal income and wealth, but they were also generous benefactors which benefited the less well-off. Were they alive today, I believe they would all be supporters of a massive dose of devolution across all aspects of society, seeking smaller, more local, more generalist, and therefore more responsive organisations. This would encompass not only industry and commerce, but also health, welfare and political governance. This would encourage experimentation with different approaches, out of which the best would survive.

Let us revisit the thinking of the Lunar Men, of their contemporary adventurers and innovators, and of such philosophers as Malthus and Pareto, and apply it in today's global circumstances. Along the way, let us give Sir Francis Galton credit, not only for his remarkable achievements in exploration, statistics, meteorology, fingerprints, heredity and psychology, but also for his creation of a framework of considerate and patient eugenics. Let us recognise him as one of the most outstanding thinkers of his generation, with messages that are highly relevant today.

Ironically, if this comes to pass, he will no longer be *The Forgotten Brummie!*